Rick Steves'
SNAPSHOT

Dublin

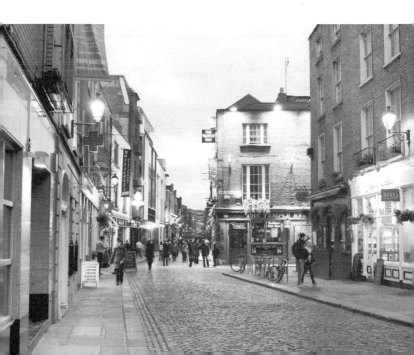

CONTENTS

INTRODUCTION

This Snapshot guide, excerpted from my guidebook *Rick Steves' Ireland,* introduces you to the city of Dublin. From its lively pubs filled with Guinness-fueled craic (conversation) and traditional music, to its stately Georgian sights, to its powerful rebel history, the Irish capital delights its visitors. Stroll vibrant O'Connell Street for a lesson in Ireland's long struggle for independence, cheer on the local hurling team at Croke Park, and pore over the intricately decorated ninth-century Book of Kells. Pious, earthy, witty, brooding, feisty, and unpretentious, Dublin is an intoxicating potion to sip or slurp—as the mood strikes you.

For a break from the big city, venture to sights near Dublin: the prehistoric tombs at Brú na Bóinne, the site of the pivotal Battle of the Boyne, the stout ruins of Trim Castle, the impressive Gardens of Powerscourt, the monastic settlement at Glendalough, and the proud Irish equestrian tradition at the National Stud.

To help you have the best trip possible, I've included the following topics in this book:

• **Planning Your Time,** with advice on how to make the most of your limited time

• **Orientation,** including tourist information (abbreviated as TI), tips on public transportation, local tour options, and helpful hints

• **Sights** with ratings:

▲▲▲—Don't miss

▲▲—Try hard to see

▲—Worthwhile if you can make it

No rating—Worth knowing about

• **Sleeping and Eating,** with good-value recommendations in every price range

• **Connections,** with tips on trains, buses, and driving

• **Practicalities,** near the end of this book, has information on money, phoning, hotel reservations, transportation, and more.

To travel smartly, read this little book in its entirety before you go. It's my hope that this guide will make your trip more meaningful and rewarding. Traveling like a temporary local, you'll get the absolute most out of every mile, minute, and dollar.

Happy travels!

Rick Steves

DUBLIN

With reminders of its stirring history and rich culture on every corner, Ireland's capital and largest city is a sightseer's delight. Dublin holds its own above its weight class in arts, entertainment, food, and fun. Dublin's fair city will have you humming, "Cockles and mussels, alive, alive-O."

Founded as a Viking trading settlement in the ninth century, Dublin grew to be a center of wealth and commerce, second only to London in the British Empire. Dublin, the seat of English rule in Ireland for 750 years, was the heart of a "civilized" Anglo-Irish area (eastern Ireland) known as "the Pale." Anything "beyond the Pale" was considered uncultured and almost barbaric...purely Irish.

The Golden Age of English Dublin was the 18th century. The British Empire was on a roll, and the city was right there with it. Largely rebuilt during this Georgian era, Dublin—even with its tattered edges—became an elegant and cultured capital.

Those glory days left a lasting imprint on the city. Squares and boulevards built in the Georgian style give the city an air of grandeur ("Georgian" is British for Neoclassical...named for the period when four consecutive King Georges occupied the British throne from 1714 to 1830). The National Museum, the National Gallery, and many government buildings are in the Georgian section of town. Few buildings (notably Christ Church and St. Patrick's cathedrals) survive from before this Georgian period.

But nationalism—and a realization of the importance of human rights—would forever change Dublin. The American and French revolutions inspired Irish intellectuals to buck British rule, and life in Dublin was never quite the same after the Rebellion of 1798. In 1801, the Act of Union with Britain resulted in the loss of Ireland's parliament (no need for two with the dominant one in London). As the Irish members of parliament moved to Westminster, the movers and shakers of the Anglo-Irish aristocracy followed suit, and Dublin slowly began to decay.

Throughout the 19th century, as Ireland endured the Great Potato Famine and saw the beginnings of the modern struggle for independence, Dublin was treated—and felt—more like a British colony than a partner. The tension culminated in the Easter Uprising of 1916, soon followed by a successful guerilla war of independence against Britain and Ireland's tragic civil war. With many of its grand streets left in ruins, Dublin emerged as the capital of the British Empire's only former colony in Europe.

While bullet-pocked buildings and dramatic statues keep memories of Ireland's struggle for independence alive, the city is looking ahead to a brighter future. Dubliners are energetic and helpful, while visitors enjoy a big-town cultural scene wrapped in a small-town smile.

Planning Your Time

On all but the shortest trips, Dublin deserves three nights and two days. Be aware that some important sights close on Mondays. Consider this ambitious sightseeing plan:

Day 1

10:15 Take the Trinity College guided walk.

11:00 Visit the Book of Kells and Old Library ahead of midday crowds.

12:00 Browse Grafton Street, have lunch there or picnic on St. Stephen's Green.

13:30 Head to the National Museum: Archaeology branch (closed Mon).

15:00 See Number Twenty-Nine Georgian House (reserve guided tour ahead of time, closed Sun-Mon).

17:00 Return to hotel, rest, have dinner—eat well for less during early-bird specials.

19:30 Go for an evening guided pub tour (musical or literary).

22:00 Drop in on Irish music in the Temple Bar area.

Day 2

10:00 Take the Dublin Castle tour.

11:30 Hop on one of the hop-on, hop-off buses, jumping off to see the Guinness Storehouse and Kilmainham Gaol (bring a sandwich to munch in transit on the open-top bus, or stop off to picnic in one of Dublin's green squares).

15:00   Leave the bus at Parnell Square, visit the Garden of Remembrance, and stroll down to O'Connell Bridge, sightseeing and shopping as you like along the way.

Evening   Catch a play or concert—or try the storytelling dinner at The Brazen Head.

With More Time: Dublin, while relatively small, can keep you busily sightseeing for days without even leaving the center of town. And with all its music, theater, and after-hours tours—not to mention the lively pub scene—evenings are just as fun.

Orientation to Dublin

Greater Dublin sprawls with 1.3 million people—more than a quarter of the country's population. But the center of tourist interest is a tight triangle be-tween O'Connell Bridge, St. Stephen's Green, and Christ Church Cathedral. Within or near this triangle, you'll find Trinity College (Book of Kells), a cluster of major museums (including the top choice, the National Museum: Archaeology branch), Grafton Street (top pedestrian shopping zone), Temple Bar (trendy and touristy nightlife center), Dublin Castle, and the hub of most city tours and buses. The only major sights outside this easy-to-walk triangle are the Kilmainham Gaol, the Guinness Storehouse, and the National Museum: Decorative Arts and History branch (all west of the center).

The River Liffey cuts the town in two. Focus on the southern half, where most of your sightseeing will take place. Dublin's wide main drag, O'Connell Street, starts north of the river at the Parnell monument and runs south, down to the central O'Connell Bridge. After crossing the bridge, this major city axis changes its name to Westmoreland and continues south, past Trinity College and through pedestrian-only Grafton Street to St. Stephen's Green.

Get used to the fact that many long Dublin streets change their names every few blocks. A prime example of this: the numerously named quays (pronounced "keys") that run east-west along the River Liffey.

The suburban port of Dun Laoghaire (dun LEERY) lies south of Dublin, 25 minutes away by DART commuter train. Travelers looking for a mellow town to sleep in outside of urban Dublin can easily home-base here. Another option is the northern suburb of

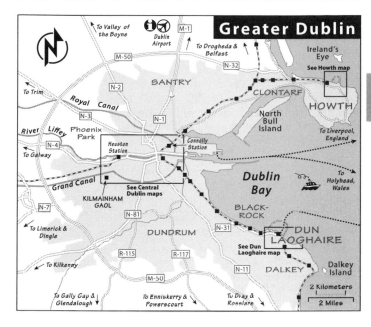

Howth, also 25 minutes away on DART and closer to the airport. Room prices are about one-quarter cheaper in Dun Laoghaire or Howth than in downtown Dublin.

Tourist Information

Dublin's **main TI** is a thriving hub of ticket and info desks filling an old church (June-Sept Mon-Sat 9:00-17:30, Oct-May Mon-Sat 9:30-17:30, Sun 10:30-15:00 year-round, a block off Grafton Street on Suffolk Street, tel. 01/850-230-330 or 01/605-7700, www.visitdublin.com). It has a bus-info desk, sandwich bar, more maps than you'll ever need, and racks advertising the busy entertainment scene. You can buy tickets to many theater and concert events here. It's also a good place to pick up brochures for destinations throughout Ireland. There's another TI at the **airport** (daily 8:00-20:00, Terminal 1). A smaller satellite TI is halfway down the east side of **O'Connell Street** (Mon-Sat 9:00-17:00, closed Sun).

At any TI, you can pick up *The Guide,* which includes a decent city map (free). Inside is a minimal schedule of happenings in town. The excellent *Collins Illustrated Discovering Dublin Map* (€7 at TIs and newsstands) is the ultimate city map, listing just about everything of interest, along with helpful opinions and tidbits of Dublin history.

Dublin Pass: This sightseeing pass is a good deal only if you like to visit lots of sights quickly (€35/1 day, €55/2 days, €65/3 days, €95/6 days, sold at TIs, www.dublinpass.ie). The pass saves a few minutes, when you'd otherwise need to wait in line to buy a ticket. It covers 34 museums, churches, literature-related sights, and expensive stops such as the Guinness Storehouse and the Old Jameson Distillery, plus the Aircoach airport bus—one-way from the airport to the city only (doesn't cover Airlink buses). However, the pass doesn't include the famous Book of Kells at Trinity College and gives only minor discounts on some bus tours and walking tours. Most travelers won't get their money's worth out of this pass.

Arrival in Dublin
By Train
Dublin has two train stations. **Heuston Station,** on the west end of town, serves west and southwest Ireland (45-minute walk from O'Connell Bridge; take the LUAS light rail or bus #90—see below). **Connolly Station,** which serves the north, northwest, and Rosslare, is closer to the center (15-minute walk from O'Connell Bridge). Each station has ATMs, but no lockers.

The two train stations are connected by the red line of the LUAS light rail system and by bus. Bus #90 runs along the river, linking the train stations, bus station, and city center (€1.80, 6/hour).

To reach Heuston Station from the city center, catch bus #90 on the south side of the river; to get to Connolly Station and Busáras Central Bus Station from the city center, catch #90 on the north side of the river.

By Bus
Bus Éireann, Ireland's national bus company, uses the **Busáras Central Bus Station** (pronounced bu-SAUR-us...like a dinosaur). Located next to Connolly Station, it's a 10-minute walk or a short ride on bus #90 (described above) to the city center.

By Plane
Dublin Airport has two terminals. Terminal 2 serves American carriers (Delta, United, American, and US Airways), plus most Aer Lingus flights. Terminal 1 serves Ryanair, Aer Arann, Air Canada, Aer Lingus (some regional flights), and most European carriers, including British Airways, SAS, Lufthansa, Air France, Swiss Air, and Iberia (airport code: DUB, tel. 01/814-1111, www.dublinairport.ie).

Both terminals, located an easily walkable 150 yards apart, have ATMs, exchange bureaus, cafés, Wi-Fi, and luggage storage. At Terminal 1, the left-luggage office (daily 6:00-23:00) is across the street in the Short-Term Car Park Atrium, along with a small supermarket. Terminal 1 also has a TI (daily 8:00-20:00), pharmacy, bus-and-rail info desk, and car-rental agencies (on ground/arrivals level).

Getting Downtown by Bus: You have two main choices—Airlink (double-decker green bus) or Aircoach (single-deck blue bus). Both pick up on the street directly in front of airport arrivals, at ground level at both terminals. Consider buying a **Rambler** city-bus pass at the airport TI (€6.90/1 day, €15/3 days, €25/5 days), which covers the Airlink bus into town—but read the following description first to make sure Airlink is the best choice for your trip.

Airlink: Airlink bus #747 stops at both airport terminals, linking the airport to the city center along a strip a few blocks north and south of the river. The route includes the Busáras Central Bus Station, Connolly Station, O'Connell Street, Trinity College, Christ Church, and Heuston Station. Ask the driver which stop is closest to your hotel (€6, pay driver, 3/hour, 35-45 minutes, tel. 01/873-4222, www.dublinbus.ie).

Aircoach: To reach recommended hotels near St. Stephen's Green (south of the city center), the Aircoach bus is best (€8, covered by Dublin Pass, 3/hour, runs 5:00-23:30, pay driver and confirm best stop for your hotel, tel. 01/844-7118, www.aircoach.ie).

City Bus: The cheapest (and slowest) way from the airport to downtown Dublin is by city bus; buses marked #16A, #41, #41A, and #41B go to O'Connell Street (€2.40, exact change required, no change given, 4/hour, 55 minutes, tel. 01/873-4222, www.dublinbus.ie).

Getting to Dun Laoghaire by Bus: The best way to get to Dun Laoghaire is to take the **Aircoach** bus (€9, hourly, 50 minutes, tel. 01/844-7118, www.aircoach.ie).

Taking a Taxi: Taxis from the airport into Dublin cost about €25; to Dun Laoghaire, about €35; to Howth, about €20.

By Ferry

Coming from the UK, you have two choices. **Irish Ferries** has four sailings per day arriving at Dublin Port at the mouth of the River Liffey (two miles east of the town center). **Stena Line** also has four sailings per day, three arriving at Dublin Port and one at Dun Laoghaire (does not run off-season, easy DART train connections to and from Dublin).

By Car

Trust me: You don't want to drive in downtown Dublin. Cars are unnecessary for sightseeing in town, parking is expensive (about €25/day), and traffic will get your fighting Irish up. Save your car-rental days for cross-country travel between smaller towns and see this energetic city by taxi, bus, or on foot. If you have a car, sleep out in the suburbs (Dun Laoghaire or Howth), and ask your inn-keeper about the best places to park.

Drivers renting a car at Dublin Airport but not staying in Dun Laoghaire or Howth can bypass the worst of the big-city traffic by taking the M-50 ring road south or west. The M-50 uses an auto-matic tolling system called eFlow. Your rented car should come with an eFlow tag installed; confirm this when you pick up your car at the airport. The €3 toll per trip is automatically debited from the credit card that you used to rent the car (for pass details, see www.eflow.ie).

Note: Your rental car's eFlow tag will only work automatically for the M-50. On any other Irish toll roads (there aren't many), you'll have to pay with cash (under €3).

Helpful Hints

High Costs: Despite the demise of the Celtic Tiger economic boom (1995-2007—R.I.P.), Ireland is still one of the EU's more expensive countries. Restaurants and lodging—other than hostels—are more expensive the closer you get to the touristy Temple Bar district. A pint of beer in a Temple Bar pub costs €5 (a sobering thought).

Pickpockets: Irish destinations, especially Dublin, are not im-mune to this scourge. Wear a money belt or risk spending a couple of days of your cherished vacation in bureaucratic purgatory—on the phone canceling credit cards and at the embassy waiting for a replacement passport (see below). Wasting vacation time this way is like paying to wait in line at the DMV.

Tourist Victim Support Service: This service can be helpful if you run into any problems (Mon-Sat 10:00-18:00, Sun 12:00-18:00, tel. 01/478-5295, www.itas.ie).

Festivals: Book ahead during festivals and for any weekend. St. Patrick's Day is a four-day March extravaganza in Dublin (www.stpatricksday.ie). June 16 is Bloomsday, dedicated to the Irish author James Joyce and featuring the Messenger Bike Rally (www.jamesjoyce.ie). Hotels raise their prices and are packed on rugby weekends (about four per year), during the all-Ireland Gaelic football and hurling finals (Sundays in Sep-tember), and during summer rock concerts.

Meet a Dubliner: The **City of a Thousand Welcomes** offers a free service that brings together volunteers and first-time visitors for a cup of tea or a pint. Visitors sign up online in advance, pick an available time slot, and meet their Dublin "ambassador" at the Little Museum of Dublin on St. Stephen's Green. You'll head for a nearby tearoom or pub and enjoy a short, informal conversation to get you oriented to the city (free, must be at least 21, 15 St. Stephens Green, tel. 01/661-1000, mobile 087-131-7129, www.cityofathousandwelcomes.com).

DUBLIN

Internet Access: Internet cafés are plentiful. **Viva Internet** is close to Christ Church Cathedral (Mon-Thu 10:00-22:00, Fri-Sat 10:30-22:00, Sun 12:00-22:00, Lord Edward Street near City Hall, tel. 01/672-4725). **Central Internet Café** is aptly named (Mon-Fri 9:00-22:00, Sat 11:00-19:00, Sun 12:00-18:00, 6 Grafton Street, easy-to-miss door is directly opposite AIB Bank, tel. 01/677-8298, www.centralinternetcafe.com). **Global Internet Café** is north of the River Liffey (Mon-Fri 8:00-21:00, Sat 9:00-20:00, Sun 10:00-20:00, 8 Lower O'Connell Street, tel. 01/878-0295).

Bookstores: The giant granddaddy of them all is **Eason's,** five minutes north of the O'Connell Bridge (Mon-Sat 8:30-18:30, Sun 12:00-17:30, 40 Lower O'Connell Street, tel. 01/858-3800). South of the River Liffey, check out the intimate **Bookstore Upstairs,** 50 yards from the front gate of Trinity College (Mon-Fri 10:00-19:00, Sat 10:00-18:00, Sun 14:00-18:00, 36 College Green, tel. 01/679-6687).

Laundry: Krystal Launderette, a block southwest of Jurys Inn Christ Church on Patrick Street, is full-service only. Allow six hours and about €10 for a load (Mon-Fri 9:00-20:00, Sat 9:00-18:00, closed Sun, tel. 01/473-1779). The **All-American Launderette** offers self and full service options (Mon-Sat 8:30-19:00, Sun 10:00-18:00, 40 South Great George's Street, tel. 01/677-2779).

Bike Rental: Phoenix Park Bike Hire offers a stress-free ride option in huge, 1,750-acre Phoenix Park. It's located off Chesterfield Avenue, the main road bisecting the park, at the closest corner of the park to the city center, roughly across the river from Heuston Station (€5/hour, €10/3 hours, €20/day, daily 10:00-19:00 "weather depending," mobile 086-265-6258, www.phoenixparkbikehire.com).

Updates to this Book: For updates to this book, see www.ricksteves.com/update.

Getting Around Dublin

You'll do most of Dublin on foot, though when you need public transportation, you'll find it readily available and easy to use. With a little planning, sightseers can make excellent use of a two-day hop-on, hop-off bus ticket to link the best sights.

By Bus: Public buses are cheap and cover the city thoroughly. Most lines start at the four quays, or piers, that are nearest

O'Connell Bridge. If you're away from the center, nearly any bus takes you back downtown. Some bus stops are "request only" stops: Be alert to the bus numbers (above the windshield) of approaching buses. When you see your bus coming, hold your arm out from your side with your palm extended into the street to flag it down. Tell the driver where you're going, and he'll ask for €1.65-2.80 depending on the number of stops. Bring change or lose any excess. Bus #90 connects the bus and train stations (see "Arrival in Dublin— By Train," earlier).

The bus office at 59 Upper O'Connell Street has free bus-route maps and sells two different city-bus passes (Mon 8:30-17:30, Tue-Fri 9:00-17:30, Sat 9:00-14:00, Sun 9:30-14:00, tel. 01/873-4222, www.dublinbus.ie). The three-day **Rambler pass** is handiest for the average traveler's stay, costing €15 and covering the Airlink airport bus (but not Aircoach buses or DART trains). The one-day **Short Hop pass,** which costs €12, includes DART trains (but not Airlink or Aircoach buses). Passes are also sold at TIs, newsstands, and markets citywide (mostly Centra, Mace, Spar, and Londis).

By DART (Train): Speedy commuter trains run along the coast, connecting Dublin with Dun Laoghaire's ferry terminal (south of city), Howth's harbor (north of city), and recommended B&Bs. Think of the DART line as a giant "C" that serves coastal suburbs from Bray in the south to Howth in the north (€2.80, €5.25 round-trips valid same day only, Eurail Pass valid if you use a counted flexi-day, tel. 01/703-3504, www.irishrail.ie/home).

By LUAS (Light Rail): The city's light-rail system has two main lines (red and green) that serve inland suburbs. The more useful line for tourists is the red line, with an east-west section connecting the Heuston and Connolly train stations (a 15-minute ride apart) at opposite edges of the Central 1 Zone. In between, the Busáras Central Bus Station, Smithfield, and Museum stops can be handy (€1.60, 6/hour, runs 5:30-24:45, tel. 1-800-300-604, www.luas.ie). Check the 15-foot-high pillars at each boarding platform that display the time and destination of the next LUAS train. Make sure you're on the right platform for the direction you want to go.

By Taxi: Taxis are everywhere and easy to hail (cheaper for 3-4 people). In recent years, Dublin has acquired a glut of new cabbies who are fiercely competing for fewer customers due to the economic downfall. Cabbies are generally honest, friendly, and good sources of information (€4.10 daytime minimum 8:00-20:00, €4.45 nighttime minimum 20:00-8:00, €1 for each additional adult, figure about €12 for most crosstown rides, €40/hour for guided joy-ride).

Tours in Dublin

While Dublin's physical treasures are lackluster by European standards, the gritty city has a fine story to tell and people with a natural knack for telling it. It's a good town for walking tours, and the competition is fierce. Pamphlets touting creative walks are posted all over town. Choices include medieval walks, literary walks, Georgian Dublin walks, traditional music pub crawls, and even a rock-and-stroll walk tracing the careers of contemporary Irish bands. Taking an evening walk is a great way to meet other travelers. The Dublin TI also offers series of free, good-quality "iWalks" for travelers with smartphones or tablets (download with maps at www.visitdublin.com). There's also a Visit Dublin app.

By Foot

▲▲Historical Walking Tour

This is your best introductory walk. A group of hardworking history graduates—many of whom claim to have done more than just kiss the Blarney Stone—enliven Dublin's basic historic strip (Trinity College, Old Parliament House, Dublin Castle, and Christ Church Cathedral). You'll get the story of their city, from its Viking origins to the present. Guides speak at length about the roots of Ireland's struggle with Britain. As you listen to your guide, you'll stand in front of buildings that aren't much to look at, but are lots to talk about (May-Sept daily at 11:00 and 15:00, April and Oct daily at 11:00, Nov-March Fri-Sun only at 11:00). All walks last two hours and cost €12 (get the €10 "student" discount rate with this book in 2014, free for kids under 14, departs from front gate of Trinity College, private tours available, mobile 087-688-9412 or 087-830-3523, www.historicalinsights.ie).

▲▲▲Traditional Irish Musical Pub Crawl

This impressive and entertaining tour visits the upstairs rooms of three pubs; there, you'll listen to two musicians talk about, play, and sing traditional Irish music. While having only two musicians makes the music a bit thin (Irish music aficionados will say you're better off just finding a good session), the evening—though touristy—is not gimmicky. It's an education in traditional Irish music. The musicians

clearly enjoy introducing rookies to their art and are very good at it. Humor is their primary educational tool. In the summer, this popular tour frequently sells out—reserve ahead (€12, €1 discount with this book, beer extra, allow 2.5 hours, April-Oct daily at 19:30, Nov-March Thu-Sat only, maximum 50 tourists, meet upstairs at Gogarty's Pub at the corner of Fleet and Anglesea in the Temple Bar area, tel. 01/475-3313, www.musicalpubcrawl.com).

▲Dublin Literary Pub Crawl

Two actors take 40 or so tourists on a walk, stopping at four pubs. Their clever banter introduces the novice to the high *craic* of James Joyce, Seán O'Casey, and W. B. Yeats. The two-hour tour is punctuated with 20-minute pub breaks (free time). While the beer lubricates the social fun, it dilutes the content of the evening. (If you want straight lit and drama, find a real performance; there are many throughout the summer, such as the lunchtime hour on weekends at 13:00 at the Dublin Writers Museum.) However, the pub crawl is an easygoing excuse to drink beer in busy pubs, hook up with other travelers, and get a dose of Irish witty lit (€12, April-Oct daily at 19:30, Nov-March Thu-Sun at 19:30; you can normally just show up, but call ahead in July-Aug when it can fill up; meet upstairs in the Duke Pub—off Grafton on Duke Street, tel. 01/670-5602, mobile 087-263-0270, www.dublinpubcrawl.com). Connoisseurs of Irish pubs will want to buy the excellent *Dublin Literary Pub Crawl* guidebook by pub-crawl founder Colm Quilligan.

1916 Rebellion Walking Tour

This two-hour walk breathes gritty life into the most turbulent year in modern Irish history, when idealistic Irish rebels launched the Easter Uprising—eventually leading to independence from Britain. Guide Lorcan Collins has written a guidebook called *The Easter Rising*—worth seeking out—and is passionate about his walks (€12, €2 discount with this book in 2014, daily March-Oct Mon-Sat at 11:30, Sun at 13:00, no tours Nov-Feb, departs from International Bar at 23 Wicklow Street, mobile 086-858-3847, www.1916rising.com).

Pat Liddy's Walking Tours

Pat Liddy is one of Dublin's top historians. He and his guides take groups on enthusiastic and informal 1.5-hour walks of hidden Dublin districts. Unlike most Dublin walks, this one does a good job of covering the often overlooked but historic north side of town. You'll start near the General Post Office building, wind down across the river to City Hall, through Temple Bar, and end at Trinity College (€10, April-Oct Mon-Sat at 11:00 and 14:30, Sun at 11:00, meet in front of the Dublin Bus Office at 59 Upper O'Connell Street, tel. 01/832-9406, mobile 087-905-2480, www. walkingtours.ie).

Rebel Tours of Dublin

These 1.5-hour walks (within a six-block area between Parnell Square and the General Post Office) focus on revolutionary events in Dublin from 1913 to 1923, when Ireland shed British rule. Strongly opinionated, these guides view history through the lens of Irish Republicanism (€10, departs Mon-Sat at 11:30 from Sinn Fein Bookshop at 58 Parnell Square, book ahead by phone, tel. 01/814-8542).

By Bike

Dublin City Bike Tours

You'll "get your *craic* on a saddle" with Dublin City Bike Tours as you pedal across this flat city on innovative urban bikes. Their fun tours visit 20 points of interest north and south of the River Liffey, covering more ground (five miles) than walking tours. Designed for riders of average fitness, they set a casual pace, and rarely let a little rain stop them (€24 includes bike, helmet, snack, and water; €4 discount with this book—show when you pay, cash only, reserve in advance, 2.5 hours, March-Nov daily at 10:00, additional tours Fri and Sat at 14:00, custom tours available for groups of 8 or more, departs Isaac's Hostel a half-block west of Busáras Central Bus Station at 2-5 Frenchman's Lane, mobile 087-134-1866, www.dublincitybiketours.com).

By Bus (on Land and Water)

▲Hop-on, Hop-off Bus Tours

Two companies (Dublin Bus Tour and City Sightseeing Dublin) offer hop-on, hop-off bus tours of Dublin, doing virtually identical 1.5-hour circuits. You can get on or off at your choice of about 20 stops (€18, 4/ hour, daily 9:00-17:00— Dublin Bus Tour until 18:30, buy ticket on board, valid for 2 days). Buses are double-deckers (roofless is fun on dry days), with  live running commentaries. **Dublin Bus Tour** (green buses) drivers provide fun and quirky narration (tel. 01/703-3028, www.dublinsightseeing.ie). **City Sightseeing Dublin** (red buses) come with both a guide and a driver, rather than just a driver who guides (tel. 01/898-0700, www.irishcitytours.com). Tickets are valid for two consecutive days—not 48 hours from the time you buy it. To make the most of it, buy your ticket early in the day.

This type of tour is made-to-order for Dublin, and buses run so frequently that they make your sightseeing super-efficient.

Stops include the far-flung Guinness Storehouse and Kilmainham Gaol. Each company's map, free with your ticket, details various discounts that you'll get at Dublin's sights (such as the Guinness Storehouse, Viking Splash tour, Old Jameson Distillery, Dublin Writers Museum, Dublinia, Christ Church Cathedral, and others). To take advantage of the discounts, take a bus tour before you do all your sightseeing.

▲Viking Splash Tours

If you'd like to ride in a WWII amphibious vehicle—driven by a Viking-costumed guide who's as liable to spout history as he is to growl—this is for you. The tour starts with a group roar from the Viking within us all. At first, the guide talks as if he were a Viking ("When we came here in 841..."), but soon the patriot emerges as he tags Irish history onto the sights you pass. Near the end of the 1.25-hour tour (punctuated by occasional group roars at passersby), you don a life jacket for a slow spin up and down a boring canal. The covered boat is breezy—dress appropriately. Kids who expect a Viking splash may feel like they've been trapped in a classroom, while historians will enjoy the talk more than the gimmick (€20, Feb-Nov daily 10:00-17:00, no tours Dec-Jan, departs about hourly from the north side of St. Stephen's Green opposite Dawson Street, buy ticket from driver, tel. 01/707-6000, www.vikingsplash.com).

Weekend Tour Packages for Students

Andy Steves (Rick's son) runs **WSA Europe**, offering three-day and longer tour packages—including accommodations, sightseeing, and local experiences—for budget travelers in top European cities including Dublin (from €99, www.wsaeurope.com).

Self-Guided Walk

▲▲O'Connell Street Stroll

Dublin's grandest street leads from O'Connell Bridge through the heart of north Dublin. Since the 1740s, it has been a 45-yard-wide promenade, and ever since the first O'Connell Bridge connected it to the Trinity side of town in 1794, it's been Dublin's main drag. (It was only named O'Connell after independence in 1922.) These days, the city has made the street more pedestrian-friendly, and a new LUAS line extension will eventually run within the median. Though lined with fast-food joints and souvenir shops, O'Connell Street echoes with history.

• *Start your walk on the...*

O'Connell Bridge: This bridge, worth ▲▲, spans the River Liffey, which historically has divided the wealthy, cultivated south side of town from the poorer, cruder north side. While there's plenty of culture above the river, even today "the north" is considered rougher and less safe. Dubliners joke that north-side residents are known as "the accused," while residents on the south side are addressed as "your honor."

From the bridge, look upriver (west) as far upstream as you can. On the left in the distance, the **big concrete building**—nicknamed "the bunker" and considered an eyesore by locals—houses the city planning commission. Ironically, it's in charge of new building permits. It squats on the still-buried precious artifacts of the first Viking settlement, established in Dublin in the ninth century. Archaeologists were given minimal time to study the dig before officials paved paradise and put up a parking lot (actually the Dublin City Council offices).

Across the river from that stands the **Four Courts**—the Supreme Court building. It was shelled and burned in 1922 during the tragic civil war that followed Irish independence. The national archives office burned, and irreplaceable birth records were lost, making it more difficult today for those with Irish roots to trace their ancestry.

The closest bridge upstream—the elegant iron **Ha' Penny Bridge**—leads into the Temple Bar nightlife district. Just beyond that old-fashioned, 19th-century bridge is Dublin's pedestrian **Millennium Bridge,** inaugurated in 2000. (Note that buses leave from O'Connell Bridge—specifically Aston Quay—for the Guinness Storehouse and Kilmainham Gaol.)

Turn 180 degrees and look downstream to see the tall **Liberty Hall** union headquarters (16 stories tall, some say in honor of the 1916 Easter Uprising). Modern Dublin is developing downstream. During the Celtic Tiger boom, the Irish (forever clever tax fiddlers) subsidized and revitalized this formerly dreary quarter. A short walk downstream along the north bank leads to a powerful series of gaunt statues memorializing the Great Potato Famine of 1845-1849. Beyond, you'll see the masts of the *Jeanie Johnston,* a replica transport ship.

• *Now start north up O'Connell Street, walking on the wide, tree-lined median strip.*

Statues and Monuments: The median is dotted with statues celebrating great figures from Ireland's past—particularly the century (c.1830-1930) when Ireland rediscovered its roots and won its independence. At the base of the street stands the man for whom Dublin's main street is named—**Daniel O'Connell** (1775-1847). He was known as the "Liberator" for founding the Catholic Association and demanding Irish Catholic rights in the British Parliament. He organized thousands of nonviolent protestors into so-called "monster meetings," whose sheer size intimidated the British authorities.

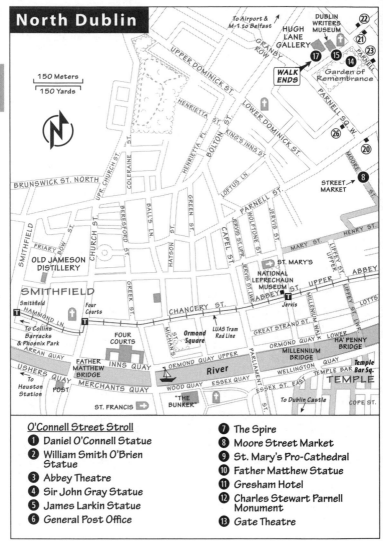

North Dublin

150 Meters
150 Yards

O'Connell Street Stroll

1. Daniel O'Connell Statue
2. William Smith O'Brien Statue
3. Abbey Theatre
4. Sir John Gray Statue
5. James Larkin Statue
6. General Post Office

7. The Spire
8. Moore Street Market
9. St. Mary's Pro-Cathedral
10. Father Matthew Statue
11. Gresham Hotel
12. Charles Stewart Parnell Monument
13. Gate Theatre

Farther along is **William Smith O'Brien,** O'Connell's protégé and leader of the Young Ireland Movement, who was imprisoned and exiled. At Abbey Street, a block detour east leads to the famous **Abbey Theatre,** where turn-of-the-century nationalists (including the poet-playwright W. B. Yeats) staged Irish-themed plays. The original building suffered a fire and was rebuilt into a nondescript, modern building, but it's still the much-loved home of the Irish National Theatre.

• *Continue up O'Connell Street.*

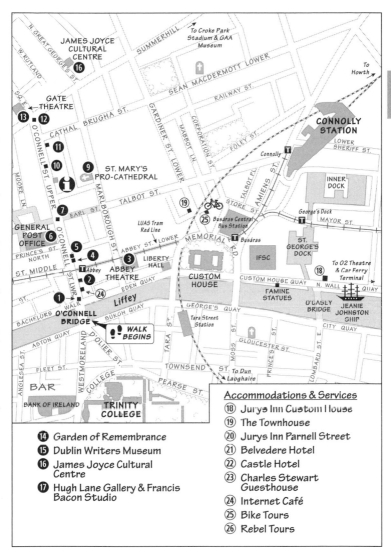

DUBLIN

Accommodations & Services
- ⑱ Jurys Inn Custom House
- ⑲ The Townhouse
- ⑳ Jurys Inn Parnell Street
- ㉑ Belvedere Hotel
- ㉒ Castle Hotel
- ㉓ Charles Stewart Guesthouse
- ㉔ Internet Café
- ㉕ Bike Tours
- ㉖ Rebel Tours

- ⑭ Garden of Remembrance
- ⑮ Dublin Writers Museum
- ⑯ James Joyce Cultural Centre
- ⑰ Hugh Lane Gallery & Francis Bacon Studio

Look for the statue of **Sir John Gray,** who, as a newspaperman and politician, was able to help O'Connell's cause. The statue of **James Larkin,** arms outstretched, honors the founder of the Irish Transport Workers Union.

• *On your left is the...*

General Post Office: This is not just any P.O. It was from here that Patrick

Pearse read the Proclamation of Irish Independence in 1916, kicking off the Easter Uprising. The building itself—a kind of Irish Alamo—was the rebel headquarters and scene of a bloody five-day siege that followed the proclamation. The post office was particularly strategic because it housed the main telegraph node for the entire country. Its pillars are still pockmarked with bullet holes (open for business and sightseers Mon-Sat 8:00-20:00, closed Sun).

Tucked in the ground floor of the building is the small **An Post Museum,** which stamp collectors and Irish rebels at heart will enjoy (€2, Mon-Fri 10:00-17:00, Sat 10:00-16:00, closed Sun, last entry 30 minutes before closing, on the right as you enter, www.anpost.ie/historyandheritage).

• *Stand at the intersection of O'Connell and Henry streets, at the base of the can't-miss-it...*

Spire: There used to be a monument here that didn't wave an Irish flag—a tall column crowned by a statue of the British hero of Trafalgar, Admiral Horatio Nelson. It was blown up in 1966—the IRA's contribution to the local celebration of the Easter Uprising's 50th anniversary. The spot is now occupied by The Spire: 390 feet of stainless steel. While it trumpets rejuvenation on its side of the river, it's a memorial to nothing and has no real meaning. Dubious Dubliners call it the tallest waste of €5 million in all of Europe. Its nickname? Take your pick: the Stiletto in the Ghetto, the Stiffy on the Liffey, the Pole in the Hole, the Poker near the Croker (after nearby Croke Park), or the Spike in the Dike.

• *Turn west (left) down people-filled Henry Street (Dubliners' favorite shopping lane), then wander to the right into the nearby...*

Moore Street Market: Many merchants here have staffed the same stalls for decades. Start a conversation. It's a great workaday scene. You'll see lots of mums with strollers—a reminder that Ireland is one of Europe's youngest countries, with more than 35 percent of the population under the age of 25 (Mon-Sat 8:00-18:00, closed Sun).

• *Return to O'Connell Street. A block east (right) of O'Connell, down Cathedral Street, detour to...*

St. Mary's Pro-Cathedral: Although this is Dublin's leading Catholic church, it rather curiously isn't a "cathedral." The pope declared Christ Church to be a cathedral in the 12th century—and later, gave St. Patrick's the same designation. (The Vatican has chosen to stubbornly ignore the fact that Christ Church and St.

Patrick's haven't been Catholic for centuries.) Completed in 1821, this Neoclassical church is in the style of a Greek temple.

• *Back on O'Connell Street, head up the street (north) until you find the statue of...*

Father Matthew: A leader of the temperance movement of the 1830s, Father Matthew was responsible, some historians claim, for enough Irish peasants staying sober to enable Daniel O'Connell to organize them into a political force. (Perhaps studying this example, the USSR was careful to keep the price of vodka affordable.)

Nearby, the fancy **Gresham Hotel** is a good place for an elegant tea or beer. In an earlier era, the beautiful people alighted here during visits to Dublin. In the 1960s, Richard Burton and Liz Taylor stayed at the hotel while he was filming *The Spy Who Came In from the Cold*. (In those days, parts of Dublin were drab enough to pass for an Eastern Bloc city.)

• *Standing boldly at the top of O'Connell Street is a monument to...*

Charles Stewart Parnell: Ringing the monument are the names of the four ancient provinces of Ireland and all 32 Irish counties (including North and South, since this was erected before Irish independence). It's meant to honor Charles Stewart Parnell (1846-1891), the member of Parliament who nearly won Home Rule for Ireland in the late 1800s (and who served time at Kilmainham Gaol). A Cambridge-educated Protestant of landed-gentry stock, Parnell envisioned a modern, free Irish nation of Catholics—but not set up as a religious state. The Irish people, who remembered their grandparents' harsh evictions during

the famine, came to love Parnell (despite his privileged birth) for his tireless work to secure fair rents and land tenure. Momentum seemed to be on his side. With the British prime minister of the time, William Gladstone, favoring a similar form of Home Rule, it looked as if Ireland was on its way toward independence as a Commonwealth nation, similar to Canada or Australia. Then a sex scandal broke around Parnell and his mistress, the wife of another Parliament member. The press, egged on by the powerful Catholic bishops (who didn't want a secular, free Irish state), battered away at the scandal until finally Parnell was driven from office. Sadly, after that, Ireland became mired in the Troubles of the 20th century: an awkward independence (1921) featuring a divided island, a bloody civil war, and sectarian violence for decades afterward. Wracked with exhaustion and only in his mid-40s, Parnell is thought to have died of a broken heart.

DUBLIN

• *Continue straight up Parnell Square East. At the* **Gate Theatre** *(on the left), Orson Welles and James Mason had their professional acting debuts. One block up, on the left, is the...*

Garden of Remembrance: Honoring the victims of the 1916 Uprising, the park was dedicated in 1966 on the 50th anniversary

of the revolt that ultimately led to Irish independence. The bottom of the cross-shaped pool is a mosaic of Celtic weapons, symbolic of how the early Irish proclaimed peace by breaking their weapons and throwing them into a lake or river. The Irish flag flies above the park: green for Catholics, orange for Protestants, and white for the hope that they can live together in peace.

One of modern Ireland's most stirring moments occurred here in May of 2011, when Queen Elizabeth II made this the first stop on her historic visit to Ireland. She laid a wreath at the *Children of Lir* sculpture under this flag and bowed her head in silence out of respect for the Irish rebels who had fought and died trying to gain freedom from her United Kingdom. This was a hugely cathartic moment for both nations. Until this visit, no British monarch had set foot in the Irish state since its founding 90 years earlier (free, daily 8:30-18:00).

• *Your walk is over. Two excellent museums are nearby, standing side-by-side: the Dublin Writers Museum (in a splendidly restored Georgian mansion) and the art-filled Hugh Lane Gallery. Here at the north end of town, it's also convenient to visit the Gaelic Athletic Association Museum at Croke Park Stadium (a 20-minute walk or short taxi ride away). Otherwise, hop on your skateboard and zip back to the river.*

Sights in Dublin

South of the River Liffey

Trinity College

Founded in 1592 by Queen Elizabeth I to establish a Protestant way of thinking about God, Trinity has long been Ireland's most prestigious college. Originally, the student body was limited to rich Protestant men. Women were admitted in 1903, and Catholics—though allowed entrance by the school much earlier—were only given formal permission by the Catholic Church to study at Trinity in the 1970s. Today, half of Trinity's 12,500 students are women, and 70 percent are culturally Catholic (although only about 20 percent of Irish youth are churchgoing).

▲▲Trinity College Tour

Trinity students organize and lead 30-minute **tours** of their campus (look just inside the gate for posted departure times and a ticket seller on a stool). You'll get a rundown of the mostly Georgian architecture; a peek at student life past and present;

and the enjoyable company of your guide, a witty Irish college kid.

Cost and Hours: €10, includes €9 fee to see Book of Kells (where the tour leaves you), May-Sept daily 10:15-15:40, Feb-April and Oct-Nov Sat-Sun only, no tours Dec-Jan, departs roughly every 30 minutes, weather permitting.

▲▲Book of Kells in the Trinity Old Library

The Book of Kells—a 1,200-year-old version of the gospels of the Bible—was elaborately inked and meticulously illustrated by faithful monks. Combining Christian symbols and pagan styles, it's a snapshot of medieval Ireland in transition. Arguably the finest piece of art from what is generally called the Dark Ages, the Book of Kells shows that monastic life in this far fringe of Europe was far from dark.

Cost and Hours: €9 (included in Trinity College tour admission—see earlier), audioguide-€5, Mon-Sat 9:30-17:00, Sun 9:30-16:30 (Oct-April Sun 12:00-16:30), tel. 01/896-2320, www.tcd.ie/library/bookofkells.

Crowd-Beating Tips: Lines are longest at midday (roughly 11:00-14:30). Ideally, queue up before the library opens to have the Book of Kells to yourself.

Visiting the Library: Your visit has three stages: 1) an exhibit on the making of the Book of Kells, including videos, old manuscripts, and poster-sized reproductions of its pages (your best look at the book's detail); 2) the Treasury, the darkened room containing the Book of Kells itself and other, less-ornate contemporaneous volumes; and 3) the main chamber of the Old Library (called the Long Room), containing historical objects.

Background: The Book of Kells was a project by Irish monks cloistered on the remote Scottish island of Iona. They slaughtered 185 calves, soaked the skins in lime, scraped off the hair, and dried the skins into a cream-colored writing surface called vellum. Only then could the tonsured monks pick up their swan-quill pens and get to work.

The project may have been underway in 806 when Vikings savagely pillaged and burned Iona, killing 68 monks. The survivors

DUBLIN

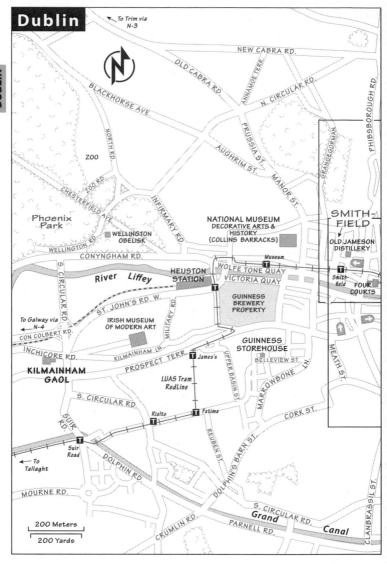

fled to the Abbey of Kells (near Dublin). Scholars are still debating exactly where the book was produced: It could have been made entirely at Iona or at Kells, or started in Iona and finished at Kells.

For eight centuries, the glorious gospel sat regally atop the high altar of the monastery church at Kells, where the priest would read from it during special Masses. In 1654, as Cromwell's ravaging armies approached, the book was smuggled to Dublin for safety. Here at Trinity College, it was first displayed to the public

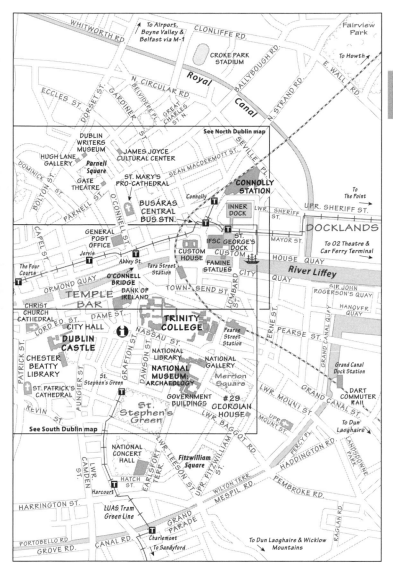

in the mid-1800s. In 1953, the book got its current covers and was bound into four separate volumes. The 1,200-year journey of the Book of Kells reached its culmination in 2012, when it came out as an iPad app.

The Exhibit: The first-class "Turning Darkness into Light" exhibit, with a one-way route, puts the 680-page illuminated manuscript in its historical and cultural context, preparing you to see the original book and other precious manuscripts in

Dublin at a Glance

▲▲▲**Traditional Irish Musical Pub Crawl** A fascinating, practical, and enjoyable primer on traditional Irish music. **Hours:** April-Oct daily at 19:30, Nov-March Thu-Sat only. See page 11.

▲▲▲**National Museum: Archaeology** Interesting collection of Irish treasures from the Stone Age to today. **Hours:** Tue-Sat 10:00-17:00, Sun 14:00-17:00, closed Mon. See page 27.

▲▲▲**Kilmainham Gaol** Historic jail used by the British as a political prison—today a museum that tells a moving story of the suffering of the Irish people. **Hours:** Mon-Sat 9:30-16:30, Sun 10:00-16:30. See page 52.

▲▲**Historical Walking Tour** Your best introduction to Dublin. **Hours:** May-Sept daily at 11:00 and 15:00, April and Oct daily at 11:00, Nov-March Fri-Sun only at 11:00. See page 11.

▲▲**Trinity College Tour** Ireland's most famous school, best visited with a 30-minute tour led by one of its students. **Hours:** Departs every 30 minutes May-Sept daily 10:15-15:40, Feb-April and Oct-Nov Sat-Sun only, no tours Dec-Jan; weather permitting. See page 21.

▲▲**Book of Kells in the Trinity Old Library** An exquisite illuminated manuscript, the most important piece of art from the Dark Ages. **Hours:** Mon-Sat 9:30-17:00, Sun 9:30-16:30 (Sun 12:00-16:30 Oct-April). See page 21.

▲▲**Grafton Street** The city's liveliest pedestrian shopping mall. **Hours:** Always open. See page 36.

▲▲**Dublin Castle** The city's historic 700-year-old castle, featuring ornate English state apartments, tourable only with a guide. **Hours:** Mon-Sat 10:00-16:45, Sun 12:00-16:45. See page 38.

▲▲**Chester Beatty Library** American expatriate's eclectic yet sumptuous collection of literary and religious treasures from Islam, the Orient, and medieval Europe. **Hours:** Mon-Fri 10:00-17:00, Sat 11:00-17:00, Sun 13:00-17:00; closed Mon Oct-April. See page 39.

▲▲**Temple Bar** Dublin's trendiest neighborhood, with shops, cafés, theaters, galleries, pubs, and restaurants—a great spot for live traditional music. **Hours:** Always open. See page 44.

▲▲**O'Connell Bridge** Landmark bridge spanning the River Liffey at the center of Dublin. **Hours:** Always open. See page 14.

DUBLIN

▲▲O'Connell Street Dublin's grandest promenade and main drag, packed with history and ideal for a stroll. **Hours:** Always open. See page 14.

▲Number Twenty-Nine Georgian House Restored 18th-century house; tours provide a glimpse of middle-class Georgian life. **Hours:** Tue-Sat 10:00-17:00, closed Sun-Mon and mid-Dec-mid-Feb. See page 35.

▲National Gallery Fine collection of top Irish painters and European masters. **Hours:** Mon-Sat 9:30-17:30, Thu until 20:30, Sun 12:00-17:30. See page 34.

▲Merrion Square Enjoyable and inviting park with a fun statue of Oscar Wilde. **Hours:** Always open. See page 35.

▲St. Stephen's Green Relaxing park surrounded by fine Georgian buildings. **Hours:** Always open. See page 38.

▲Dublinia A fun, kid-friendly look at Dublin's Viking and medieval past with a side order of archaeology and a cool town model. **Hours:** Daily March-Sept 10:00-17:00, Oct-Feb 11:00-16:30. See page 43.

▲Dublin Writers Museum Modest collection of authorial bric-a-brac. **Hours:** June-Aug Mon-Fri 10:00-18:00, Sat 10:00-17:00, Sun 11:00-17:00; Sept-May Mon-Sat 10:00-17:00, Sun 11:00-17:00. See page 45.

▲Hugh Lane Gallery Modern and contemporary art, starring Monet, Bacon, and Irish artists. **Hours:** Tue-Thu 10:00-18:00, Fri-Sat 10:00-17:00, Sun 11:00-17:00, closed Mon. See page 48.

▲Guinness Storehouse The home of Ireland's national beer, with a museum of beer-making, a gallery of clever ads, and Gravity Bar with panoramic city views. **Hours:** Daily 9:30-17:00, July-Aug until 19:00. See page 52.

▲National Museum: Decorative Arts and History Shows off Irish dress, furniture, silver, and weaponry with a special focus on the 1916 rebellion, fight for independence, and civil war. **Hours:** Tue-Sat 10:00-17:00, Sun 14:00-17:00, closed Mon. See page 54.

▲Gaelic Athletic Association Museum High-tech museum of traditional Gaelic sports such as hurling and Irish football. **Hours:** Daily 9:30-17:00, Sun 11:30-17:00. On game Sundays, it's open only to ticket holders. See page 54.

DUBLIN

the treasury. Make a point to spend time in the exhibit (before reaching the actual Book of Kells). Especially interesting are the five-minute video clips showing the exacting care that went into transcribing the monk-uscripts and the ancient art of bookbinding. Two small TV screens (on opposite walls of the exhibition room) run continuously, silently demonstrating the monks' labors of love.

The Book: The Book of Kells contains the four gospels of the Bible. It's 680 pages long (or 340 "folios," the equivalent of one sheet, front and back). The Latin calligraphy—all in capital letters—follows ruled lines, forming neat horizontal bars across the page. Sentences end with a "period" of three dots. The black-brown ink was made from the galls of oak trees. Scholars have found a number of spelling errors that were never corrected, apparently because the look was more important than accuracy.

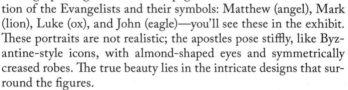

The text is elaborately decorated—of the 680 pages, only two are without decoration. Each gospel begins with a full-page illustration of the Evangelists and their symbols: Matthew (angel), Mark (lion), Luke (ox), and John (eagle)—you'll see these in the exhibit. These portraits are not realistic; the apostles pose stiffly, like Byzantine-style icons, with almond-shaped eyes and symmetrically creased robes. The true beauty lies in the intricate designs that surround the figures.

The colorful book employs blue, purple, red, pink, green, and yellow pigments (all imported)—but no gold leaf. Letters and borders are braided together. On most pages, the initial letters are big and flowery, like in a children's fairytale book. The entire Chi-Rho page is dedicated to just the letters "XP" (the first two letters of Christ's name in Greek), made into an elaborate maze of interlacing lines.

Elsewhere, the playful monks might cross a "t" with a fish, form an "h" from a spindly-legged man, or make an "e" out of a coiled snake. Animals crouch between sentences. It's a jungle of intricate designs, inhabited by tiny creatures both real and fanciful, with no two the same—humans, angels, gargoyles, dragons, wolves, calves, and winged lions.

Stylistically, the monks mixed Christian symbols (the cross, fish, peacock, snake) with pagan motifs (spirals, key patterns, knotwork; some swirls are similar to those seen on the carved stones at Newgrange). The designs are also reminiscent of the jewelry of the day, with its ornate filigree patterns studded with knobs (like the Tara Brooch).

Scholars think three main artists created the book: the "gold-smith" (who did the filigree-style designs), the "illustrator" (who specialized in animals and grotesques), and the "portrait painter" (who did the Evangelists and Mary). Some of the detail work is unbelievably minute—akin to drawing a Persian carpet on the tiny face of a dice. Did the monks use a magnifying glass? There's no evidence they had such strong lenses.

The Old Library: The Long Room, the 200-foot-long main chamber of the Old Library (from 1732), is stacked to its towering ceiling with 200,000 books. Among the displays here, you'll find one of a dozen surviving original copies of the **Proclamation of the Irish Republic.** Patrick Pearse read out its words at Dublin's General Post Office on April 24, 1916, starting the Easter Uprising that led to Irish independence. Notice the inclusive opening phrase ("Irishmen and Irishwomen") and the seven signatories (each of whom was executed).

Another national icon is nearby: the oldest surviving Irish **harp,** from the 15th century (sometimes called the Brian Boru harp). The brass pins on its oak and willow frame once held 29 strings. These weren't mellifluous catgut strings, like those on a modern harp, but wire strings that made a twangy sound when plucked. In Celtic days, poets—the equal of kings and Druid priests—wandered the land, uniting the people with songs and stories. The harp's inspirational effect on Gaelic culture was so strong that Queen Elizabeth I (1558-1603) ordered Irish harpists to be hung and their instruments smashed. Even today, the love of music is so intense that Ireland is the only country with a musical instrument as its national symbol. You'll see this harp's likeness everywhere, including on the back of Irish euro coins, on government documents, and on every pint of Guinness.

▲▲▲National Museum: Archaeology

Showing off the treasures of Ireland from the Stone Age to modern times, this branch of the National Museum is itself a national treasure. The soggy marshes and peat bogs of Ireland have proven perfect for preserving old objects. You'll see 4,000-year-old gold jewelry, 2,000-year-old bog mummies, Viking swords, and the collection's superstar—the exquisitely wrought Tara Brooch. Visit here to get an introduction to the rest of Ireland's historic attractions: You'll find a reconstructed passage tomb like Newgrange, Celtic art like the Book of Kells, Viking objects from Dublin, a model of the Hill of Tara, and a sacred cross from the Cong Abbey. Hit the highlights of my tour, then browse at will, aided by good posted information.

Cost and Hours: Free, Tue-Sat 10:00-17:00, Sun 14:00-17:00, closed Mon, guided tours offered sporadically (€2, mostly weekends, call in morning or check website), €2 audioguide covers only Treasury room, good café, between Trinity College and St. Stephen's Green on Kildare Street, tel. 01/677-7444, www.museum.ie.

● **Self-Guided Tour:** On the ground floor, enter the main hall. In the center (down four steps) are displays of prehistoric gold jewelry. To the left are the bog bodies, to the right is the Treasury, and upstairs is the Viking world. We'll start at Ireland's beginning.

❶ **Stone Age Tools:** Glass cases hold flint and stone axeheads and arrowheads (7,000 B.C.). Ireland's first inhabitants—hunters and fishers who came from Scotland—used these tools. These early people also left behind standing stones (dolmens) and passage tombs.

❷ **Reconstructed Passage Tomb:** At the corner of the room, you'll see a typical tomb circa 3,000 B.C.—a mound-shaped, heavy stone structure, covered with smaller rocks, with a passage leading into a central burial chamber where the deceased's ashes were interred. This is a modest tomb; the vast passage tombs at Newgrange and Knowth are 20 times bigger.

❸ **The Hill of Tara:** The famous passage-tomb burial site at Tara, known as the Mound of the Hostages, was used for more than 1,500 years as a place to inter human remains. The cases in this side gallery display some of the many exceptional Neolithic and Bronze Age finds uncovered at the site.

Over the millennia, the Mound became the very symbol of Irish heritage. This is where Ireland's kings claimed their power, where St. Patrick preached his deal-clinching sermon, and where, in the 1800s, Daniel O'Connell rallied Irish patriots to demand their independence from Britain.

❹ **The Evolution of Metalworking:** Around 2500 B.C., Ireland discovered how to make metal—mining ore, smelting it in furnaces, and casting or hammering it into shapes. The rest is prehistory. You'll travel through the Bronze Age (axeheads from 2000 B.C.) and Iron Age (500 B.C.) as you examine assorted spears, shields, swords, and war horns. The cauldrons made for everyday cooking were also used ceremonially to prepare elaborate ritual feasts for friends and symbolic offerings for the gods. The most impressive metal objects are in the center of the hall.

❺ **Ireland's Gold:** Ireland had modest gold deposits, mainly gathered by prehistoric people panning for small nuggets and dust in the rivers. But the jewelry they left, some of it more than 4,000 years old, is exquisite. The earliest fashion choice was a

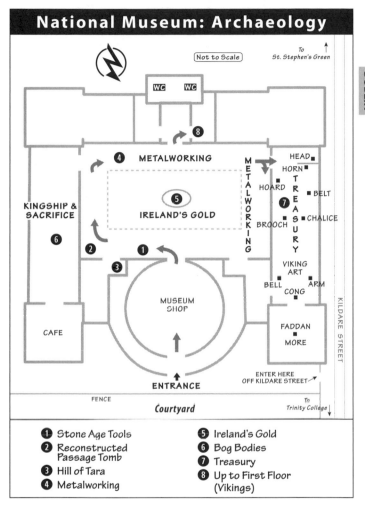

National Museum: Archaeology

Not to Scale

To St. Stephen's Green

WC WC

❹ METALWORKING

METALWORKING

HEAD ■
HORN ■

T
R
E
A
S
U
R
Y

HOARD
❼ BELT ■

❺
IRELAND'S GOLD

BROOCH

CHALICE ■

KINGSHIP & SACRIFICE

❻

❷

❶

❸

VIKING ART

BELL ARM ■
CONG ■

MUSEUM SHOP

FADDAN ■
MORE

CAFE

ENTER HERE
OFF KILDARE STREET →

KILDARE STREET

ENTRANCE

FENCE

Courtyard

To Trinity College

❶ Stone Age Tools
❷ Reconstructed Passage Tomb
❸ Hill of Tara
❹ Metalworking

❺ Ireland's Gold
❻ Bog Bodies
❼ Treasury
❽ Up to First Floor (Vikings)

broad necklace hammered flat (a *lunula*, so called for its crescent-moon shape). This might be worn with accompanying earrings and sun-disc brooches. Later jewelry (c. 800 B.C.) was cast from clay molds into bracelets and unique "dress fasteners" that you'd slip into buttonholes to secure a cloak. Some of these gold objects may have been gifts to fertility gods, offered by burying them in marshy bogs.

❻ **Bog Bodies:** When the Celts arrived in Ireland (c. 500 B.C.-A.D. 500), they brought with them a mysterious practice: They brutally murdered sacrificial slaves or prisoners and buried them in bogs. Several bodies—shriveled and leathery, but remarkably pre-

Modern Ireland's Turbulent Birth: A Timeline

Imagine if our American patriot ancestors had fought both our Revolutionary War and our Civil War over a span of seven chaotic years...and then appreciate the remarkable resilience of the Irish people. Here's a summary of what happened when.

1916: A nationalist militia called the Volunteers (led by **Patrick Pearse**) and the socialist Irish Citizen Army (led by **James Connolly**) join forces in the **Easter Uprising**, but they fail to end 750 years of British rule. The uprising is unpopular with most Irish, who are unhappy with the destruction in Dublin and preoccupied with the "Great War" on the Continent. But when 16 rebel leaders (including Pearse and Connolly) are executed, Irish public opinion reverses as sympathy grows for the martyrs and the cause of Irish Independence.

Two important rebel leaders escape execution. New York-born **Eamon de Valera** is spared because of his American passport (the British don't want to anger their potential ally in World War I). **Michael Collins,** a low-ranking rebel officer who fought in the uprising at the General Post Office, refines urban guerrilla-warfare strategies in prison, and then blossoms after his release as the rebels' military and intelligence leader in the power vacuum that followed the executions.

1918: World War I ends and a general election is held in Ireland. Outside of Ulster, the nationalist **Sinn Fein** party wins 73 out of 79 seats in Parliament. Only 4 out of 32 counties vote to maintain the Union with Britain (all 4 are in Ulster, part of which would become Northern Ireland). Rather than take their seats in London, Sinn Fein representatives abstain from participating in a government they see as foreign occupiers.

1919: On January 19, the abstaining Sinn Fein members set

served—have been dug up from around the Celtic world (in the British Isles and Northern Europe).

Clonycavan Man is from Ireland. One summer day around 200 B.C., this twentysomething man was hacked to death with an axe and disemboweled. In his time, he stood 5'9" tall and had a mohawk-style haircut, poofed up with pine-resin hair product imported from France. Today you can still see traces of his hair. Only his upper body survived; the lower part may have been lost in the threshing machine that unearthed him in 2003.

up a rebel government in Dublin called Dail Eireann. On the same day, the first shots of the **Irish War of Independence** are fired as rebels begin ambushing police barracks, which are seen as an extension of British rule. De Valera is elected by the Dail to lead the rebels, with Collins as his deputy. Collins' web of spies infiltrates British intelligence at Dublin Castle. The Volunteers rename themselves the **Irish Republican Army;** meanwhile the British beef up their military presence in Ireland by sending in tough WWI vets, the Black and Tans. A bloody and very personal war ensues.

1921: Having lived through the slaughter of World War I, the British tire of the extended bloodshed in Ireland and begin negotiations with the rebels. De Valera leads rebel negotiations, but then entrusts them to Collins (a clever politician, de Valera sees that whoever signs a treaty will be blamed for its compromises). Understanding the tricky position he's been placed in, Collins signs the **Anglo-Irish Treaty** in December, lamenting that in doing so he has signed his "own death warrant."

The Dail narrowly ratifies the treaty (64 to 57), but Collins' followers are unable to convince de Valera's supporters that the compromises are a stepping stone to later full independence. De Valera and his anti-treaty disciples resign in protest. **Arthur Griffith,** founder of Sinn Fein, assumes the presidential post.

In June, the anti-treaty forces, holed up in the Four Courts building, are fired upon by Collins and his pro-treaty forces—thus igniting the **Irish Civil War.** The British want the treaty to stand and even supply Collins with cannons, meanwhile threatening to re-enter Ireland if the anti-treaty forces aren't put down.

1922: In August, Griffith dies of stress-induced illness, and Collins is assassinated 10 days later. Nevertheless, the pro-treaty forces prevail, as they are backed by popular opinion and better (British-supplied) military equipment.

1923: In April, the remaining IRA forces dump (or stash) their arms, ending the civil war...but many of their bitter vets vow to carry on the fight. De Valera distances himself from the IRA and becomes the dominant Irish political leader for the next 40 years.

Why were these people killed? It appears to have been a form of ritual human sacrifice of high-status people. Some may have been enemy chiefs or political rivals, but regardless, their deaths were offerings to the gods to ensure rich harvests and good luck. Other items (now on display) were buried along with them—gold bracelets, royal cloaks, and finely wrought cauldrons.

❼ **Treasury:** Irish metalworking is legendary, and this room holds 1,500 years of exquisite objects. Working from one end of the long room to the other, you'll journey from the world of the pagan

Celts to the coming of Christianity, explore the stylistic impact of the Viking invasions (9th-12th century), and consider the resurgence of ecclesiastical metalworking (11th-12th century).

Pagan Era Art: A mysterious pagan god greets you, in a **carved stone head** from circa A.D. 100. The god's three faces express the different aspects of his stony personality. This abstract style—typical of Celtic art—would be at home in a modern art museum. A **bronze horn** (first century B.C.) is the kind of curved war trumpet that the Celts blasted to freak out the Roman legions. The fine objects of the **Broighter Hoard** (first century B.C.) include a king's golden collar decorated in textbook Celtic style, with interlaced vines inhabited by stylized faces. The tiny boat was an offering to the sea god. The coconut-shell-shaped bowl symbolized a cauldron. By custom, the cauldron held food as a constant offering to Danu, the Celtic mother goddess, whose mythical palace was at Bru na Boinne.

Early Christian Objects: Christianity officially entered Ireland in the fifth century (when St. Patrick converted the pagan king), but Celtic legends and art continued well into the Christian era. You'll see various crosses, shrines (portable reliquaries containing holy relics), and chalices decorated with Celtic motifs. The **Belt Shrine**—a circular metal casing that held a saint's leather belt—was thought to have magical properties. When placed around someone's waist, it could heal the wearer or force him or her to tell the truth.

The **Chalice of Ardagh** and the nearby **Silver Paten** were used during Communion to hold blessed wine and bread. Get close to admire the elaborate workmanship. The main bowl of the chalice is gilded bronze, with a contrasting band of intricately patterned gold filigree. It's studded with colorful glass, amber, and enamels. Mirrors below the display case show that even the underside of the chalice was decorated. When the priest grabbed the chalice by its two handles and tipped it to his lips, the base could be admired by God.

Tara Brooch: A rich eighth-century Celtic man fastened his cloak at the shoulder with this elaborate ring-shaped brooch, its seven-inch stick-pin tilted rakishly upward. Made of cast and gilded silver, it's ornamented with fine, exquisitely filigreed gold panels and studded with amber, enamel, and colored glass. The motifs include Celtic spirals, snakes, and stylized faces, but the symbolism is neither overtly pagan nor Christian—it's art for art's sake. Despite its fanciful name, the brooch probably has no actual connection to the Hill of Tara. In display cases nearby, you'll see other similar (but less impressive) brooches from the same period—some iron, some bronze, and one in pure gold.

Viking Art Styles: When Vikings invaded Dublin around

A.D. 800, they raped and pillaged. But they also opened Ireland to a vast and cosmopolitan trading empire, from which they imported hoards of silver (see the display case of ingots). Viking influence shows up in the decorative style of reliquaries like the **Lismore Crozier** (in the shape of a bishop's ceremonial shepherd's crook) and the **Shrine of St. Lochter's Arm** (raised in an Irish-power salute). The impressive **Bell of St. Patrick** was supposedly owned by Ireland's patron saint. After his death, it was encased within a beautifully worked shrine (displayed alongside) and kept safe by a single family, who passed it down from generation to generation for 800 years.

Cross of Cong: "By this cross is covered the cross on which the Creator of the world suffered." Running along the sides of the cross, this Latin inscription tells us that it once held a sacred relic, a tiny splinter of the True Cross on which Jesus was crucified. That piece of wood (now lost) had been given in 1123 to the Irish high king, who commissioned this reliquary to preserve the splinter (it would have been placed right in the center, visible through the large piece of rock crystal). Every Christmas and Easter, the cross was fitted onto a staff and paraded through the abbey at Cong, then placed on the altar for High Mass. The extraordinarily detailed decoration features gold filigree interspersed with colored glass, enamel, and (now missing) precious stones. Though fully Christian, the cross has Celtic-style filigree patterning and Viking-style animal heads (notice how they grip the cross in their jaws).

Before leaving the Treasury and heading upstairs, check out the **Faddan More Psalter**—a (pretty beat-up) manuscript of the Book of Psalms from the same era as the Book of Kells.

❶ **Viking Ireland** (c. 800-1150, on first floor): Dublin was born as a Viking town. Sometime after 795, Scandinavian warriors rowed their long ships up the Liffey River and made camp on the south bank, around the location of today's Dublin Castle and Christ Church. Over the next two centuries, they built "Duiblinn" into an important trading post, slave market, metalworking center, and the first true city in Ireland. (See a model of Dublin showing a recently excavated area near Kilmainham Gaol.)

The state-of-the-art Viking boats ("Viking" means seafarer) worked equally well in the open ocean and shallow rivers, and were perfect for stealth invasions and far-ranging trading. Soon, provincial Dublin was connected with the wider world—Scotland, England, Northern Europe, even Asia. The museum's displays of swords and spears make it clear that, yes, the Vikings were fierce warriors. But you'll also see that they were respected merchants (standardized weights and coins), herders and craftsmen (leather shoes and bags), fashion-conscious (bone combs and jewelry), fun-loving (board games), and literate (runic alphabet).

What you won't see are horned helmets, which, despite the stereotype, were not common. By 1000, the pagan Vikings had intermarried with the locals, become Christian, and were subjects of the Irish king.

The Rest of the Museum: Part of the first floor is dedicated to medieval Ireland—daily life (ploughs, cauldrons), trade (coins, pottery), and religion (crucifixes and saints). Up one more flight, the Egyptian room has coffins, shabtis, and canopic jars—but no mummies.

Other National Museums South of Trinity College

Adjacent to the archaeology branch are these other major museums. Also nearby is Leinster House. Once the Duke of Leinster's home, it now hosts the Irish Dáil (parliament) and Seanad (senate), which meet here 90 days each year.

▲National Gallery

While not as extensive as national galleries in London or Paris, the collections here are well worth your time. The museum boasts an impressive range of works by European masters, and also displays the works of top Irish painters, including Jack B. Yeats (the brother of the famous poet). Try not to miss the wonderfully romantic *Meeting on the Turret Stairs*, Ireland's favorite painting, by Frederic Burton. Because this vividly painted watercolor is vulnerable to fading, it's on view for only three hours per week (Mon and Wed 11:00-12:00 & Sat 15:00-16:00).

Cost and Hours: Free, Mon-Sat 9:30-17:30, Thu until 20:30, Sun 12:00-17:30, expect disruptions due to renovation through 2016, Merrion Square West, tel. 01/661-5133, www.nationalgallery.ie.

Tours: The museum offer a free audioguide (donations accepted) as well as free 45-minute guided tours (Sat at 12:30; Sun at 12:30, 13:30, and 14:00).

Visiting the Museum: Study the floor-plan flier and take advantage of the free audioguide. Be sure to walk the series of rooms on the ground floor devoted to Irish painting and get to know artists you may not have heard of before. Visit the National Portrait Gallery on the mezzanine level for an insight into the great personalities of Ireland. You'll find European masterworks on the top floor, including a rare Vermeer (one of only 30-some known works by the Dutch artist), a classic Caravaggio (master of chiaroscuro and dramatic lighting), a Monet riverscape, and an early Cubist Picasso still life.

National Museum: Natural History

Called "the dead zoo" by Dubliners, this cramped collection of stuffed exotic animals comes across like the locker room on Noah's Ark. But if you're into beaks, bones, bugs, and boars, this Victorian relic is for you. Standing tall above a sea of taxidermy is the regal skeleton of a giant Irish elk from the last Ice Age; it dwarfs a modern moose. The earnest displays need a new home, and a fund-raising effort is under way.

Cost and Hours: Free, Tue-Sat 10:00-17:00, Sun 14:00-17:00, closed Mon, Merrion Square West, tel. 01/677-7444, www.museum.ie.

National Library

Literature holds a lofty place in the Irish psyche. To feel the fire-and-ice pulse of Ireland's most influential poet, visit the W. B. Yeats exhibit in the library basement. This space was originally intended to host rotating exhibits, but the display on the life of Yeats proved so popular it became permanent. The artifacts flesh out the very human passions of this poet and playwright, with samples of his handwritten manuscripts and surprisingly interesting mini-documentaries of the times he lived in. Upstairs, you can get help making use of library records to trace your genealogy.

Cost and Hours: Free; Mon-Wed 9:30-19:30, Thu-Sat 9:30-17:00, closed Sun; Yeats tours Wed at 13:00 and Sat at 15:00; café, tel. 01/603-0200, 2-3 Kildare Street, www.nli.ie.

Merrion Square and Nearby

▲Merrion Square

Laid out in 1762, this square is ringed by elegant Georgian houses decorated with fine doors—a Dublin trademark. (If you're inspired by the ornate knobs and knockers, there's a shop by that name on nearby Nassau Street.) The park, once the exclusive domain of the residents, is now a delightful public escape and ideal for a picnic. To learn what "snogging" is, walk through the park on a sunny day, when it's full of smooching lovers. Oscar Wilde, lounging wittily on a boulder on the corner nearest the town center and surrounded by his clever quotes, provides a fun photo op.

▲Number Twenty-Nine Georgian House

The carefully restored house at Number 29 Lower Fitzwilliam Street gives an intimate glimpse of middle-class Georgian life (which seems pretty high-class). From the sidewalk, descend the stairs to the basement-level entrance (corner of Lower Fitzwilliam and Lower Mount Streets, opposite southern corner of Merrion Square). Start with an interesting 15-minute video before exploring this 1790 Dublin home. You'll find storyboards in each room explaining the everyday lives lived here.

DUBLIN

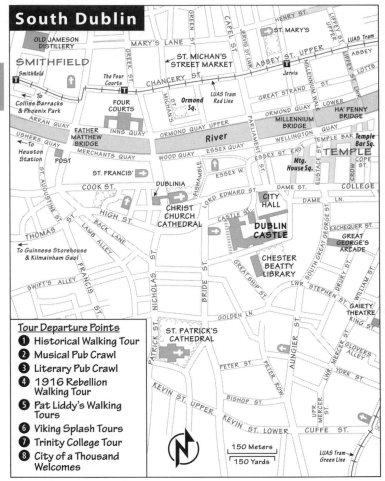

South Dublin

Tour Departure Points
1. Historical Walking Tour
2. Musical Pub Crawl
3. Literary Pub Crawl
4. 1916 Rebellion Walking Tour
5. Pat Liddy's Walking Tours
6. Viking Splash Tours
7. Trinity College Tour
8. City of a Thousand Welcomes

150 Meters
150 Yards

LUAS Tram Green Line

Cost and Hours: €6, Tue-Sat 10:00-17:00, closed Sun-Mon and mid-Dec-mid-Feb, last entry 30 minutes before closing, tours daily at 15:00, tel. 01/702-6165, www.esb.ie/no29.

Grafton Street and St. Stephen's Green Area
▲▲Grafton Street
Once filled with noisy traffic, today's Grafton Street is Dublin's liveliest pedestrian shopping mall and people-watching paradise. A decade ago, when the Celtic Tiger economy was in mid-roar, this street had the fifth-most expensive retail rents in the world, behind Tokyo, London, New York, and Moscow (rents have since declined). A 10-minute stroll past street musicians takes you from Trinity College to St. Stephen's Green (and makes you wonder

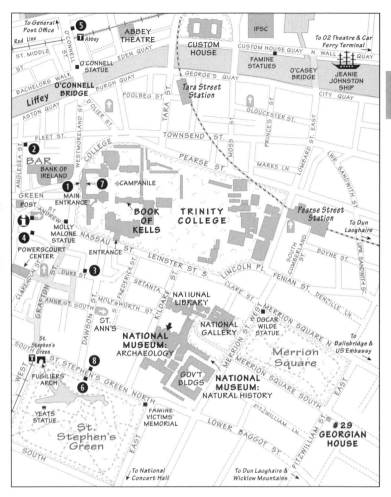

why some American merchants are so terrified of a car-free street). Walking south from Trinity College, you'll pass a buxom statue of "sweet" Molly Malone (also known as "the tart with the cart"). Next, you'll pass two venerable department stores: the Irish Brown Thomas and the English Marks & Spencer. Johnson's Court alley leads to the Powerscourt Townhouse Shopping Centre, which tastefully fills a converted Georgian mansion. The huge, glass-covered St. Stephen's Green Shopping Centre and the peaceful green itself mark the top of Grafton Street. For fun, gather a pile of coins and walk the street, setting each human statue into action with a donation. Consider stopping at the recommended Bewley's Café for coffee with a second-floor view of the action.

▲St. Stephen's Green

This city park was originally a medieval commons, complete with gory public executions. It was enclosed in 1664 and gradually surrounded with fine Georgian buildings. Today, it provides 22 acres of grassy refuge for Dubliners. At the northwest corner (near the end of Grafton Street) you'll be confronted by a looming marble arch erected to honor British officers killed during the Boer War. Locals nicknamed it "Traitor's Arch," as most Irish sympathized with the underdog Boers. On a sunny afternoon, this open space is a wonderful world apart from the big city. When marveling at the elegance of Georgian Dublin, remember that during the Georgian period, Dublin was the second-most important city in the British Empire. Area big shots knew that any money wrung from the local populace not spent in Dublin would end up in London. Since it was "use it or lose it," they used it—with gusto—to beautify their city.

Little Museum of Dublin

A fun, two-room labor of love just north of St. Stephen's Green, this collection was donated by local Dubliners and focuses on life in the city since 1900. An engaging mix of history and pop culture, this museum also sponsors the City of a Thousand Welcomes Meet a Dubliner program. Artifacts range from a first edition of James Joyce's *Ulysses* to a sticker proving that discount airline Ryanair once provided something unthinkable today—business class seating. Other displays cover local rock band U2 and Muhammad Ali's 1972 fight at Croke Park. History buffs linger at sly Eamon de Valera's five-part memo to his fellow Irish rebel Michael Collins. In part one, he gives Collins complete authority to negotiate with British officials over Irish independence—and then waters down this authority over the next four parts.

Cost and Hours: €6, daily 9:30-17:00, Thu until 20:00, tours on request, 15 St. Stephen's Green, tel. 01/661-1000, www.littlemuseum.ie.

Dublin Castle and Nearby

▲▲Dublin Castle

Built on the spot of the first Viking fortress, this castle was the seat of English rule in Ireland for 700 years. Located where the Poddle and Liffey rivers came together, making a black pool (*dubh linn* in Irish), Dublin Castle was the official residence of the viceroy who implemented the will of the British royalty. In this stirring setting, the Brits handed power over to Michael Collins and the Irish in 1922. Today, it's used for fancy state and charity functions.

Standing in the courtyard, you can imagine the ugliness of the British-Irish situation. Notice the statue of justice above the gate—pointedly without her blindfold and admiring her sword.

As Dubliners say, "There she stands, above her station, with her face to the palace and her arse to the nation." The fancy interior is viewable only with a 45-minute tour, which offers a fairly boring room-by-room walk through the lavish state apartments of this most English of Irish palaces. The tour finishes with a look at the foundations of the Norman tower and the best remaining chunk of the 13th-century town wall.

Cost and Hours: €4.50, buy tickets in courtyard under portico opposite clock tower, required tours depart hourly, Mon-Sat 10:00-16:45, Sun 12:00-16:45, tel. 01/645-8813, www.dublincastle.ie.

▲▲Chester Beatty Library

This priceless, delightfully displayed collection includes rare ancient manuscripts and beautifully illustrated books from around the world, plus a few odd curios. Start on the ground floor with the short film about Mr. Beatty (1875-1968), a rich American mining magnate who traveled widely, collected assiduously, and retired to Ireland. Then head upstairs to see the treasures he bequeathed to his adopted country.

Cost and Hours: Free, Mon-Fri 10:00-17:00, Sat 11:00-17:00, Sun 13:00-17:00, closed Mon Oct-April, coffee shop, tel. 01/407-0750, www.cbl.ie. You'll find the library in the gardens of Dublin Castle (follow the signs).

● **Self-Guided Tour:** Start on the second floor.

Sacred Traditions Gallery: This space is dedicated to sacred texts, illuminated manuscripts, and miniature paintings from around the world. The doors swing open, and you're greeted by a video highlighting a diverse array of religious rites—a Christian wedding, Muslims kneeling for prayer, whirling dervishes, and so on.

• *Tour the floor clockwise, starting with Christian texts on the left side of the room. There you'll find several glass cases containing...*

Ancient Bible Fragments: In the 1930s, Beatty acquired (possibly through the black market) these 1,800-year-old manuscripts, which had recently been unearthed in Egypt. The Indiana Jones-like discovery instantly bumped scholars' knowledge of the early Bible up a notch. There were Old Testament books (Genesis, Deuteronomy), New Testament books (Gospels, Acts, Revelation), and—rarest of all—the Letters of Paul. Written in Greek on papyrus more than a century before previously known documents, these are some of the oldest versions of these texts in existence. Unlike most early Christian texts, the manuscripts were not rolled up in a scroll but bound in a book form called a "codex." On display (the collection changes) you may see pages from a third-century Gospel of Luke or the Gospel of John (c. A.D. 150-200). Jesus died around A.D. 33, and his words weren't recorded until decades later. Most early manuscripts date from the fourth century, so these pages are about as close to the source as you can get.

Letters (Epistles) of Paul: The Beatty has 112 pages of Saint Paul's collected letters (A.D. 180-200). Paul, a Roman citizen (c. A.D. 5-67; see Albrecht Dürer's engraving of the saint), was the apostle most responsible for spreading Christianity beyond Palestine. Originally, Paul reviled Christians. But after a mystical experience, he went on to travel the known world, preaching the Good News in sophisticated Athens and the greatest city in the world, Rome, where he died a martyr to the cause. Along the way, he kept in touch with Christian congregations in cities like Corinth, Ephesus, and Rome with these letters. It's thanks to Paul that we have sayings such as "Money is the root of all evil"; "Love is patient, love is kind"; "Whatever a man sows, so shall he reap"; and "Fight the good fight."

Continuing up the left side of the room, you'll find gloriously illustrated **medieval Bibles** and **prayer books,** including an intricate, colorful, gold-speckled Book of Hours (1408).

• *Turn the corner into the center of the room, to find the sacred texts of...*

Islam: The angel Gabriel visited Muhammad (c. 570-632), instructing him to write down his heavenly visions in a book—the Quran. You'll see Qurans with elaborate calligraphy, such as one made in Baghdad in 1001. Nearby are other sacred Islamic texts, some beautifully illustrated, where you may find the rare illuminated manuscript of the "Life of the Prophet" (c. 1595), produced in Istanbul for an Ottoman sultan.

• *On the right side of the room, you enter the world of...*

East Asian Religions: Statues of Gautama Buddha (c. 563-483 B.C.) and Chinese Buddhist scrolls attest to the pervasive influence of this wise man. Buddha was born in India, but his philosophy spread to China, Japan, and Tibet (see the mandalas). Continuing clockwise, you will reach the writings from India, the land of a million gods—and the cradle of Buddhism, Hinduism, Sikhism, and Jainism.

• *Your visit continues downstairs on the first floor, in the gallery devoted to the...*

Arts of the Book: The focus here is on the many forms a "book" can take—from the earliest clay tablets and papyrus scrolls, to parchment scrolls and bound codexes, to medieval monks' wondrous illustrations, to the advent of printing and bookbinding, to the dawn of the 21st century and the digital age.

• *Tour the floor clockwise. Immediately to the left, find a glass case containing...*

Egyptian and Other Ancient Writings: A hieroglyph-covered papyrus scroll from the Book of the Dead (c. 300 B.C.) depicts a pharaoh on his throne (left) presiding over a soul's judgment in the afterlife. The jackal-headed god Anubis (center-right) holds a scale, weighing the heart of a dead woman to see if it's light enough for her to level up to the next phase of eternity. The Beatty also has a large selection of ancient Egyptian love songs (including, I believe, the number one hit of 1160 B.C., "I Love You, Mummy Dearest"). Nearby (in a freestanding glass case, near the bottom), if you look hard, you could find a few small cuneiform tablets and cylinder seals from as far back as 2,700 B.C. These objects from ancient Sumeria (modern-day Iraq) are older than the pyramids and represent the very birth of writing.

• *Continue up the left side of the room, perusing displays on...*

Printing, Illustrating, and Bookbinding: The printing press with movable type was perfected by Johannes Gutenberg in Germany sometime in the early 1450s. The printed sheets were folded, sewn together, and wrapped in a cover. With the engraving process, beautiful illustrations could also be reproduced on a mass scale. Until the 20th century, it was common for a book buyer to acquire the printed sheets and then select a lavish custom-made cover.

• *Turn the corner to the center of the room.*

Islamic World: These are secular books—science textbooks and poetry many from the rich Persian culture (modern day Iran). Some are richly illustrated with elaborate calligraphy. It's often noted that Islam forbids visual art, strictly following the Bible's dictum against "graven" images. But, as you can see, that restriction doesn't apply to non-religious texts.

• *Continue to the right side of the room.*

Far East: Besides albums and scrolls, you might see eye-catching Japanese woodblock prints, ornate Chinese snuff bottles, rhino horn cups, and the silk dragon robes of Chinese emperors of the Qing dynasty (1644-1911). The Qianlong Emperor (r. 1736-1795)—a poet and arts patron—welcomed European Jesuits to his court and commissioned a huge collection of books, including some carved from jade. A graceful Sumatran book, written on tree-bark pages, is bound so that it unfolds like an accordion—yet another example of great ingenuity in presenting the written word.

Dublin City Hall

The first Georgian building in this very Georgian city stands proudly overlooking Dame Street, in front of the gate to Dublin Castle. Built in 1779 as the Royal Exchange, it introduced the

Georgian style (then very popular in Britain and on the Continent) to Ireland. Step inside (it's free) to feel the prosperity and confidence of Dublin in her 18th-century glory days. In 1852, this building became the City Hall. Under the grand rotunda, a cycle of heroic paintings tells the city's history. (The mosaics on the floor convey such homilies as "Obedience makes the happiest citizenry.")

Pay your respects to the 18-foot-tall statue of Daniel O'Connell, the great orator and liberator who, in 1829, won emancipation for Catholics in Ireland from the much-despised Protestants over in London. The body of modern Irish rebel leader Michael Collins lay in state here after his assassination in 1922. The greeter sits like the Maytag repairman at the information desk, eager to give you more information. Downstairs is the excellent *Story of the Capital* exhibition, which has storyboards and video clips of Dublin's history.

Cost and Hours: €4, free audioguide, coffee shop, Mon-Sat 10:00-16:00, closed Sun, tel. 01/222-2204, www.dublincity.ie.

Dublin's Cathedrals Area

Because of Dublin's English past (particularly Henry VIII's Reformation, which led to the dissolution of the Catholic monasteries in both Ireland and England in 1539), neither of its top two churches is Catholic. Christ Church Cathedral and nearby St. Patrick's Cathedral are both Church of Ireland (Anglican). In the late 19th century, the cathedrals underwent extensive restoration. The rich Guinness brewery family forked out the dough to try to make St. Patrick's Cathedral outshine Christ Church—whose patrons were the equally rich, rival Jameson family of distillery fame. However, in Catholic Ireland, these Anglican sights feel hollow, and they're more famous than visit-worthy.

Christ Church Cathedral

Occupying the same site as the first wooden church built on this spot by King Sitric in late Viking times (c. 1030), the present structure is a mix of periods: Norman and Gothic, but mostly Victorian Neo-Gothic (1870s restoration work). Inside you'll find the reputed tomb of the Norman warlord Strongbow, who led the thin edge of the English military wedge that eventually dominated Ireland for centuries. This oldest building in Dublin has an unusually large underground crypt, containing stocks, statues, the cathedral's silver, and an atmospheric café.

Cost and Hours: €6 includes downstairs crypt silver exhibition, €12.25 combo-ticket includes Dublinia (described next); Mon-Sat 9:00-18:00, Sun 12:30-14:30; €4 guided tours Mon-Fri at 11:00, 12:00, 14:00, and 15:00; tel. 01/677-8099, www.christchurchdublin.ie.

Evensong: A 45-minute evensong service is sung Wed and Thu at 18:00, Sun at 15:30.

▲Dublinia

This exhibit, which highlights Dublin's Viking and medieval past, is a hit with youngsters. The exhibits are laid out on three floors. The ground floor focuses on Viking Dublin, explaining life aboard a Viking ship and inside a Viking house. Viking traders introduced urban life and commerce to Ireland—but kids will be most interested in gawking at their gory weaponry.

The next floor up reveals Dublin's day-to-day life in medieval times, from chivalrous knights and damsels in town fairs to the brutal ravages of the Plague. Like the rest of Europe at that time (1347-1349), Ireland lost one-third of its population to the Black Death. The huge scale model of medieval Dublin is especially well done.

The top floor's "History Hunters" section is devoted to how the puzzles of modern archaeology and science shed light on Dublin's history. From this floor, you can climb a couple of flights of stairs into the tower for so-so views of Dublin, or exit across an enclosed stone bridge to adjacent Christ Church Cathedral.

Cost and Hours: €7.50, €12.25 combo-ticket includes Christ Church Cathedral, daily March-Sept 10:00-17:00, Oct-Feb 11:00-16:30, last entry 45 minutes before closing, top-floor coffee shop open in summer, across from Christ Church Cathedral, tel. 01/679-4611, www.dublinia.ie.

St. Patrick's Cathedral

The first church here was built on the site where St. Patrick baptized local pagan converts. The core of the Gothic structure you see today was built in the 13th century. After the Reformation, it passed into the hands of the Anglican Church. A century later, Oliver Cromwell's puritanical Calvinist troops—who considered the Anglicans to be little more than Catholics without a pope—stabled their horses here as a sign of disrespect.

Jonathan Swift (author of *Gulliver's Travels*) was dean of the Cathedral for 32 years in the 18th century. His grave is located near the front door (on the right side of the nave), where his cutting, self-penned epitaph reads: "He lies where furious indignation can no longer rend his heart." Check out the large wooden Door of Reconciliation hanging in the north transept, with the rough hole in the middle. This was the Chapter House door through which two feuding, sword-bearing 15th-century nobles shook hands..."chancing their arms" and giving the Irish that expression of trust.

Cost and Hours: €5.50 donation to church, Mon-Fri 9:00-17:30, Sat 9:00-18:30, Sun 12:30-15:00, last entry one hour before closing.

Evensong: You'll get chills listening to the local "choir of angels" Mon-Fri at 17:45 and Sun at 15:15.

▲▲Temple Bar

This much-promoted area—with trendy shops, cafés, theaters, galleries, pubs with live music, and restaurants—feels like the heart

of the city. It's Dublin's touristy "Left Bank," and as in Paris, it's on the south shore of the river, filling the cobbled streets between Dame Street and the River Liffey.

Three hundred years ago, this was the city waterfront, where tall sailing ships offloaded their goods (a "bar" was a loading dock along the river, and the Temples were a dominant merchant family). Eventually, the city grew eastward, filling in tidal mudflats, to create the docklands of modern Dublin. Once a thriving Georgian center of craftsmen and merchants, this neighborhood fell on hard times in the 20th century. Ensuing low rents attracted students and artists, giving the area a bohemian flair. With government tax incentives and lots of development money, the Temple Bar district has now become a thriving cultural (and beer-drinking) hot spot.

Temple Bar can be an absolute spectacle in the evening, when it bursts with revelers. The noise, pushy crowds, and inflated prices have driven most Dubliners away. But even if you're just gawking, don't miss the opportunity to wander through this human circus. It can be a real zoo on summer weekend nights, holidays, and nights after big sporting events let out. Women in funky hats, part of loud "hen" (bachelorette) parties, promenade down the main drag as drunken dudes shout from pub doorways to get their attention. Be aware that a pint of beer here is at least €1 more than at less glitzy pubs just a couple of blocks away (north of the River Liffey or south of Dame Street).

Temple Bar Square, just off Temple Bar Street (near Ha' Penny Bridge), is the epicenter of activity. It hosts free street theater and a Saturday book market, and has handy ATMs. On busy weekends, people-watching here is a contact sport. You're bound to meet some characters.

Irish music fans find great CDs at Claddagh Records (Cecilia Street, just around the corner from Luigi Malone's, Mon and Wed-Sat 11:30-17:30, closed Sun and Tue, tel. 01/677-0262). Unlike big, glitzy chain stores, this is a little hole-in-the-wall shop staffed by informed folks who love turning visitors on to Irish tunes. Grab a couple of CDs for your drive through the Irish countryside. Farther west and somewhat hidden is Meeting House Square, with a lively organic-produce market (Sat 10:00-18:00). Bordering the square is the Irish Film Institute (main entry on Eustace Street), which shows a variety of art-house flicks. A bohemian crowd relaxes in its bar/café, awaiting the next film (6 Eustace Street, box office daily 13:30-21:00, tel. 01/679-5744, www.irishfilm.ie).

Rather than follow particular pub or restaurant recommendations (mine are listed later, under "Eating in Dublin"), venture

down a few side lanes off the main drag to see what looks good. The pedestrian-only **Ha' Penny Bridge,** named for the halfpence toll people used to pay to cross it, leads from Temple Bar over the River Liffey to the opposite bank and more sights. If the rowdy Temple Bar scene gets to be too much, cross over to the north bank of the River Liffey on the Millennium Pedestrian Bridge (next bridge west of the Ha' Penny Bridge), where you'll find a mellower, more cosmopolitan choice of restaurants with outdoor seating in the Millennium Walk district.

North of the River Liffey
▲Dublin Writers Museum

No other country so small has produced such a wealth of literature. As interesting to those who are fans of Irish literature as it is boring to those who aren't, this three-room museum features the lives and works of Dublin's great writers. It's a low-tech museum, where you read informative plaques while perusing display cases with minor memorabilia—a document signed by Jonathan Swift, a photo of Oscar Wilde reclining thoughtfully, an early edition of Bram Stoker's *Dracula*, a George Bernard Shaw playbill, a not-so-famous author's tuxedo, or a newspaper from Easter 1916 announcing "Two More Executions To-day." If unassuming attractions like that stir your blood—or if you simply want a manageable introduction to Irish lit—it's worth a visit.

Cost and Hours: €7.50, includes helpful audioguide; June-Aug Mon-Fri 10:00-18:00, Sat 10:00-17:00, Sun 11:00-17:00; Sept-May Mon-Sat 10:00-17:00, Sun 11:00-17:00; coffee shop, 18 Parnell Square North, tel. 01/872-2077, www.writersmuseum.com).

Background: The museum isn't exclusive about "Irish" writers. Born here? Lived here? Wrote about Ireland, wrote in Gaelic, or were sympathetic to the cause of Irish nationalism? You're in. Some of the writers featured by the museum were born in Ireland, but that's about it—they lived elsewhere, wrote in English, and gained fame for non-Irish works. One trait they all seem to share is a stubborn streak of personal independence, perhaps related to Ireland's national struggle to assert its cultural identity. The museum is housed in a Georgian home, making for an elegant setting to appreciate these pioneering writers who've left a written record of this verbal people.

Visiting the Museum: The collection is chronological. **Room 1** starts with Irish literature's deep roots in the roving, harp-playing **bards** of medieval times. By telling stories in the native language, they helped unify the island's culture. But "literature" came only with the arrival of the English language. **Jonathan Swift** (1667-1745)—Ireland's first great writer—was born in Dublin and served as dean of St. Patrick's Cathedral, though he spent much of his life in London. His stinging satire of societal hypocrisy set the tone of rebellion found in much Irish literature. The **theater** has been another longstanding Irish specialty, starting with the 18th-century playwright Oliver Goldsmith. In the **1890s,** sophisticated Dublin (and Trinity College) was a cradle for great writers who ultimately found their fortunes in England: the playwright/poet/wit Oscar Wilde, Bram Stoker (who married Wilde's girlfriend), and the big-idea playwright George Bernard Shaw. Poet **W. B. Yeats** stayed home, cultivating Irish folklore at soirees (hosted by the literary patron Lady Augusta Gregory) and inspired by his unrequited muse, the feminist Irish revolutionary Maude Gonne (see her portrait).

Room 2 continues with Yeats' **Abbey Theatre,** the scene of premieres by great Irish playwrights (including Yeats, Shaw, and Wilde), and a source of political unrest during the 1916 Easter Uprising. Dublin was also a breeding ground for bold new ideas, producing Modernist writers Samuel *(Waiting for Godot)* Beckett and James Joyce (his Cultural Centre is described next). As the 20th century progressed, playwrights such as Sean O'Casey, Brendan Behan, and Brian Friel kept Dublin at the forefront of modern theater. You can read a long letter by terrorist/bad boy Brendan Behan from Hollywood about schmoozing with Groucho, Harpo, and Sinatra.

Finish your visit by going **upstairs** to see an elegant Georgian library, then peruse the busts and portraits in the Gallery of Writers.

James Joyce Cultural Centre

Aficionados of James Joyce's work (but few others) will want to visit this micro-museum.

Cost and Hours: €5, Mon-Sat 10:00-17:00, Sun 12:00-17:00, closed Mon Oct-March, two blocks east of the Dublin Writers Museum at 35 North Great George's Street, tel. 01/878-8547, www.jamesjoyce.ie.

Background: James Joyce (1882-1941) was born and raised in Dublin, wrote in great detail about his hometown, and mined

Dublin's Literary Life

Dublin in the 1700s, grown rich from a lucrative cloth trade, was one of Europe's most cultured and sophisticated cities. The buildings were decorated in the Georgian style still visible today, and the city's Protestant elite shuttled between here and London, bridging the Anglo-Irish cultural gap. Jonathan Swift (1667-1745) was the era's greatest Anglo-Irish writer—a brilliant satirist and author of *Gulliver's Travels*. He was also dean of St. Patrick's Cathedral (1713-1745) and one of the city's eminent citizens.

Around the turn of the 20th century, Dublin produced some of the world's great modern writers. Bram Stoker (1847-1912) was creator of *Dracula*. Oscar Wilde (1854-1900) penned *The Picture of Dorian Gray* and a clutch of fine plays. George Bernard Shaw (1856-1950) wrote *Pygmalion*, *Major Barbara*, *Man and Superman*, and a host of other dramas. William Butler Yeats (1865-1939) was a prolific poet and playwright on Irish themes. And James Joyce (1882-1941) whipped up a masterpiece called *Ulysses*.

the local dialect for his pitch-perfect dialogue. His best-known work, *Ulysses*, chronicles one day in the life of the fictional Leopold Bloom (June 16, 1904) as he wanders through the underside of Dublin. In his own life, Joyce left Dublin (on June 17, 1904) to live in Paris. He never took up the cause of Irish nationalism and rarely delved into Irish mythology. His focus was the Modernist question of how to find one's place in a post-religious world without traditional guidelines. His stream-of-consciousness writing style (which, truthfully, can be hard to follow and often boring) is meant to mimic the multiple strains of thought running through a person's mind at any one moment. Joyce's frank depictions of sexuality helped employ two generations of censors in Ireland and America.

Visiting the Centre: Your visit begins (top floor) with videos on Joyce's life and his enormous influence on subsequent writers. Next, a touchscreen display traces Bloom's Dublin Odyssey. Photos of Joyce and quotes from his books decorate the walls. A re-creation of a messy, cramped study evokes Joyce's struggles through poverty and criticism as he forged his own path. Down one flight, see portraits of Joyce and his wife and muse, Nora Barnacle. (The first time they, um, went on a date was June 16, 1904.) On the ground floor, a film version of one of Joyce's short stories, *The Dead*, plays eternally. In a tiny back courtyard, you can see the original door from 7 Eccles Street, the address of Leopold Bloom.

DUBLIN

▲Hugh Lane Gallery

This collection of mostly modern and contemporary art has a sampling of Impressionist masterpieces that come from the gallery's founding collection, once owned by Sir Hugh Lane. Genteel and bite-sized, the museum is particularly worth a visit for a well-known Monet painting, an exhibit on modern artist Francis Bacon, and a few select paintings by Irish artists.

Cost and Hours: Free, Tue-Thu 10:00-18:00, Fri-Sat 10:00-17:00, Sun 11:00-17:00, closed Mon, Parnell Square North, tel. 01/222-5550, www.hughlane.ie.

Visiting the Gallery: Head to **Room 1,** where you'll find **Monet's** *Waterloo Bridge* (1900). On a visit to London, the once-bohemian, now-famous Impressionist Claude Monet checked into Room 618 of the Savoy Hotel and set to work painting Waterloo Bridge at different times of day and in various weather conditions. This painting is the best known of 41 versions of the scene. Monet—the master of capturing hazy, filtered light—loved London for its fog. With the Thames in the foreground, the bridge in the middle, and belching smokestacks in the distance, Monet had three different layers of atmospheric depth to explore.

Also in Room 1 is *Portrait of Hugh Lane* by the American society portraitist John Singer Sargent. In 1905, the dapper Sir Hugh, an art dealer, bought Monet's *Waterloo Bridge* as part of his mission to bring modern art to provincial Dublin (see a Degas painting nearby). Unfortunately, Sir Hugh went down on the *Lusitania* in 1915 and didn't see this gallery open.

Room 3 is devoted to Jack B. Yeats—the famous poet's little brother—who had a long career as a magazine illustrator, novelist, set designer for the Abbey Theatre, painter, and even Ireland's first Olympic medalist (for art). Yeats helped establish the modern movement in Ireland, and he encouraged Hugh Lane to patronize Irish artists. In his own paintings, Yeats turned to the Irish countryside and common laborers for subjects. Over time, his style evolved from realistic rural scenes to thickly painted, swirling works at the edge of abstraction. In **Room 4,** check out the next generation of Irish artists Yeats influenced—abstract and Pop Art of the 1970s and 1980s.

Francis Bacon Studio: Although he spent most of his life in London, Francis Bacon (1909-1992) was born in Dublin and raised in nearby Naas. After his death, his entire London studio was reconstructed here, just as the artist had left it.

After a wandering youth of odd jobs and petty crime, Bacon

took up painting in his late thirties. He jumped onto the art stage in 1945 with his bleak canvases of twisted, deformed, screaming-mouthed men caged in barren landscapes—which hauntingly captured the mood of post-WWII Europe. He would become Britain's premier painter, but he continued to live simply. He stayed in his small, cramped flat with an even smaller studio (this one) for his entire life. Here he painted his famous series of "Heads"—portraits of his friends, especially of his life partner, George Dyer.

The place is a mess—empty paint cans, slashed canvases, books, photos, and newspapers everywhere—leaving only enough space for Bacon to set up his canvas in the middle of it all and paint. (If I were caged here, I'd scream.) As trashed as the studio is, it reflects Bacon's belief that "chaos breeds energy."

Spend 10 minutes with the 1985 filmed interview of Bacon, which was conducted in the studio. He speaks articulately about his work and reminisces about his down-and-out days. In nearby rooms are touchscreen terminals, photos of Bacon, a few unfinished works, and display cases of personal items, such as his coffee-table book on Velázquez, the Old Master who inspired Bacon's famous portrait of a screaming pope.

National Leprechaun Museum

This good-natured, low-tech attraction is fine for kids and light-hearted adults (but too corny for teens). An uninhibited guide leads the group on a 45-minute meander through Irish mythology. You'll visit a wishing well, a giant's living room, and a fairy fort listening to tales that will enchant your wee ones.

Cost and Hours: €12, Mon-Sat 10:00-18:30, Sun 10:30-18:30, last entry 45 minutes before closing, a block north of the River Liffey on Abbey Street across from Jervis LUAS stop, tel. 01/873-3899, www.leprechaunmuseum.ie.

Evening Visits: For adults only, a one-hour evening storytelling performance goes for the darkly funny side of Irish folklore (€20, July-Aug Fri-Sat at 20:00 and 20:30).

Jeanie Johnston Tall Ship and Famine Museum

Docked on the River Liffey, this seagoing sailing ship is a replica of a legendary Irish "famine ship." The original *Jeanie Johnston* embarked on 16 six- to eight-week transatlantic crossings, carrying more than 2,500 Irish emigrants to their new lives in America and Canada in the decade after the Great Potato Famine. While many barely seaworthy hulks were known as "coffin ships," those who boarded the *Jeanie Johnston* were lucky: With a humanitarian captain and even a doctor, not one life was lost. Your tour guide will introduce you to the ship's main characters and help illuminate day-to-day life aboard a cramped tall ship 160 years ago. Because this ship makes goodwill voyages to Atlantic ports, it may be away during your visit.

Cost and Hours: €8.50, visits by 45-minute tour only, tours depart hourly, daily April-Oct 10:00-16:00, Nov-March 11:00-16:00, on the north bank of the Liffey just east of Sean O'Casey Bridge, tel. 01/473-0111, www.jeaniejohnston.ie.

Dublin's Smithfield Village

This neighborhood is worth a look for the Old Jameson Distillery whiskey tour and Dublin's most authentic traditional-music pub. The two sights are on the long Smithfield Square, two blocks northwest of the Four Courts—the Supreme Court building. The square today still fulfills its original function as a horse market (first Sat morning of the month, great for people-watching). The **Fresh Market,** near the top of the square, is a handy grocery stop for urban picnic fixings (Mon-Sat 7:00-22:00, Sun 8:00-22:00).

Old Jameson Distillery

Whiskey fans enjoy visiting the old distillery. You get a 10-minute video, a 20-minute tour, and a free shot in the pub. Unfortunately, the "distillery" feels fake and put together for tourists. The Bushmills tour in Northern Ireland (in a working factory) and the Midleton tour near Cork (in the huge original factory) are better experiences. If you do take this tour, volunteer energetically when offered the chance: This will get you a coveted seat at the whiskey taste-test table at the tour's end.

Cost and Hours: €14, 10 percent discount if booked online, daily 9:30-18:30, last tour at 17:15, Bow Street, tel. 01/807-2355, www.jamesonwhiskey.com.

Cobblestone Pub

Hiding in a derelict-looking building at the top of the square, this pub offers Dublin's least glitzy and most rewarding traditional-music venue. The candlelit walls, covered with photos of honored trad musicians, set the tone. Music is revered here, as reflected in the understated sign: "Listening area, please respect musicians."

Cost and Hours: Free, Mon-Sat 16:00-23:45, Sun 13:00-23:00, trad-music sessions Mon-Tue at 21:00, Wed-Sat at 19:00, Sun at 14:00; at north end of square, 100 yards from Old Jameson Distillery's brick chimney tower; tel. 01/872-1799, www.cobblestonepub.ie.

Outer Dublin

The Kilmainham Gaol and the Guinness Storehouse are located west of the old center and can be combined in one visit, linked by a 20-minute walk, a five-minute taxi ride, or public bus #79. (To ride the bus from the jail to the Guinness Storehouse, leave the prison and take three rights—crossing no streets—to reach the bus stop.) Another option is to take a hop-on, hop-off

From Famine to Revolution

After the Great Potato Famine (1845-1849), destitute rural Irish moved to the city in droves, seeking work and causing a housing shortage. Unscrupulous landlords came up with a solution: Subdivide the city's once-grand mansions into tiny rooms and cram poor renters into them. Dublin became one of the most densely populated cities in Europe—one of every three Dubliners lived in a slum. On Henrietta Street, once a wealthy Dublin address, these new tenements bulged with humanity. According to the 1911 census, one district counted 835 people living in 15 houses (many with a single outhouse in back or a communal chamber pot in the room). In cramped, putrid quarters like this, tuberculosis was rampant, and infant mortality skyrocketed.

Those who could get work tenaciously clung to their precious jobs. The terrible working conditions prompted many to join trade unions. A 1913 strike and employer lockout, known as the "Dublin Lockout," lasted for seven months. The picket lines were brutally put down by police in the pocket of rich businessmen, led by newspaper owner and hotel magnate William Murphy. In response, James Larkin and James Connolly formed the Irish Citizen Army, a socialist militia to protect the poor trade unionists.

Murphy eventually broke the unions. Larkin headed for the US to organize workers there. During World War I, he praised the rise of the Soviet Union and later was persecuted during the postwar "Red Scare" (even doing time in Sing Sing for advocating "unlawful means" to overthrow the US government). Meanwhile, Connolly stayed in Ireland and brought the Irish Citizen Army into the 1916 Easter Uprising as an integral part of the rebel forces. During the uprising, he slyly had a rebel flag flown over Murphy's prized hotel on O'Connell Street. The uninformed British artillery battalions took the bait and pulverized it.

Connolly was the last of the rebel leaders executed in 1916. Unable to stand in front of the firing squad in Kilmainham Gaol (his ankle was shattered by a bullet while he was defending the General Post Office), Connolly was tied to a chair and shot sitting down. Of the 16 rebel executions, his was the one most credited with turning Irish public opinion in favor of the rebel martyrs.

Today you'll find heroic Dublin statues to honor them both. James Larkin, arms outstretched, is in front of the post office on O'Connell Street. James Connolly is on Beresford Place, behind the Customs House.

bus: City Sightseeing Dublin stops right at Kilmainham Gaol, while Dublin Bus Tour stops 200 yards away, in front of the modern art museum in Kilmainham hospital. Both tours stop at the Guinness Storehouse.

▲▲▲Kilmainham Gaol (Jail)
Opened in 1796 as Dublin's county jail and a debtors' prison, Kilmainham was considered a model in its day. In reality, this jail

was frequently used by the British as a political prison. Many of those who fought for Irish independence were held or executed here, including leaders of the rebellions of 1798, 1803, 1848, 1867, and 1916. National heroes Robert Emmett and Charles Stewart Parnell each did time here. The last prisoner to be held in the jail was Eamon de Valera, who later became president of Ireland. He was released on July 16, 1924, the day Kilmainham was finally shut down. The buildings, virtually in ruins, were restored in the 1960s. Today, it's a shrine to the Nathan Hales of Ireland.

Cost and Hours: €6, Mon-Sat 9:30-16:30, Sun 10:00-16:30, last entry one hour before closing; bus #69 or #79 from Aston Quay—confirm with driver; tel. 01/453-5984. The humble cafe serves little more than sandwiches.

Visiting the Jail: Start your visit with a one-hour guided **tour** (2/hour, includes 15-minute prison-history slide show in the prison chapel—spend waiting time in museum). It's touching to tour the cells and places of execution—hearing tales of oppressive colonialism and heroic patriotism—alongside Irish schoolkids who know these names well. The museum has an excellent exhibit on Victorian prison life and Ireland's fight for independence. Don't miss the museum's dimly lit Last Words 1916 hall upstairs, which displays the stirring final letters that patriots sent to loved ones hours before facing the firing squad.

▲Guinness Storehouse
A visit to the Guinness Storehouse is, for many, a pilgrimage. Arthur Guinness began brewing the renowned stout here in 1759 and by 1868, it was the biggest brewery in the world. Today, the sprawling place fills several city blocks.

Cost and Hours: €16.50, includes a €5 pint; €1 off with your hop-on, hop-off bus ticket or 10 percent discount when you book online; daily 9:30-17:00, July-Aug until

The Famous Record-Breaking Records Book

Look up "beer" in the *Guinness World Records*, and you'll discover that the strongest brew ever sold had an alcohol volume of 55 percent (a Scottish brew called *The End of History*), and that the record for removing beer bottle caps with one's teeth is 68 in one minute. But aside from listing records for amazing—or amazingly stupid—feats, this famous record book has a more subtle connection with beer.

In 1951, while hunting in Ireland's County Wexford, Sir Hugh Beaver, then the managing director at Guinness Breweries, got into a debate with his companions over which was the fastest game bird in Europe: the golden plover or the red grouse. That night at his estate, after scouring countless reference books, they were disappointed not to find a definitive answer.

Beaver realized that similar questions were likely being debated nightly across pubs in Ireland and Britain. So he hired twins Norris and Ross McWhirter, who ran a fact-finding agency in London, to compile a book of answers to various questions. They set up an office at 107 Fleet Street and began assembling the first edition of the book by contacting experts, such as astrophysicists, etymologists, virologists, and volcanologists. In 1955, the *Guinness Book of Records* (later renamed *Guinness World Records*) was published. By Christmas, it topped the British bestseller list.

In the beginning, entries mostly focused on natural phenomena and animal oddities, but grew to include a wide variety of extreme human achievements. After more than a half-century of noting record-breaking traditions around the globe, the volume continues to answer a multitude of burning trivia questions, such as the wealthiest cat in the world, the largest burrito ever made, and the record time for peeling 50 pounds of onions (an event that likely caused a lot of tears).

The iconic books are now available in more than 100 countries and 26 languages, with more than 3.5 million copies sold annually. As the bestselling copyrighted book of all time, it even earns a record-breaking entry within its own pages.

19:00; enter on Bellevue Street, bus #123 from Dame Street and O'Connell Street; tel. 01/408-4800, www.guinness-storehouse.com.

Visiting the Brewery: Around the world, Guinness brews more than 10 million pints a day (their biggest brewery is actually in Lagos, Nigeria). Although the home of Ireland's national beer welcomes visitors with a sprawling modern museum, there are no tours of the actual working brewery.

The museum fills the old fermentation plant used from 1902

through 1988, which reopened in 2000 as a huge shrine to the tradition. Step into the middle of the ground floor and look up. A tall, beer-glass-shaped glass atrium—14 million pints big—soars upward past four floors of exhibitions and cafés to the skylight. Then look down at Arthur's original 9,000-year lease, enshrined under Plexiglas in the floor...you realize that at £45 per year, it was quite a bargain. (The brewery eventually purchased the land, so the lease is no longer valid.)

The actual exhibit makes brewing seem more grandiose than it is and treats Arthur like the god of human happiness. His pints contain only 200 calories, but they pack a 4.2 percent alcohol content. Highlights are the cooperage (with 1954 film clips showing the master keg-makers plying their now virtually extinct trade), a display of the brewery's clever ads, and a small exhibit about the beer's connection to the *Guinness World Records* (see sidebar on previous page).

Atop the building, the **Gravity Bar** provides visitors with a commanding 360-degree view of Dublin—with vistas all the way to the sea—and an included beer.

▲National Museum: Decorative Arts and History

This branch of the National Museum, which occupies the huge, 18th-century stone Collins Barracks in west Dublin, displays Irish dress, furniture, weapons, silver, and other domestic baubles from the past 700 years. History buffs will linger longest in the "Soldiers & Chiefs" exhibit, which covers the Irish at war both at home and abroad since 1500 (including the American Civil War). The sober finale is the "Understanding 1916" room, offering Ireland's best coverage of the painful birth of this nation, an event known as the "Terrible Beauty." Guns, personal letters, and death masks help illustrate the 1916 Easter Uprising, War of Independence against Britain, and Ireland's civil war. Croppies Acre, the large park between the museum and the river, was the site of Dublin's largest soup kitchen during the Great Potato Famine in 1845-1849.

Cost and Hours: Free, Tue-Sat 10:00-17:00, Sun 14:00-17:00, closed Mon, good café; on north side of the River Liffey in Collins Barracks on Benburb Street, roughly across the river from Guinness Storehouse, easy to reach by the LUAS red line—get off at Museum stop; tel. 01/677-7444, www.museum.ie. Call ahead for sporadic tour times.

▲Gaelic Athletic Association Museum

The GAA was founded in 1884 as an expression of an Irish cultural awakening. It was created to foster the development of Gaelic sports, specifically Gaelic football and hurling, and to exclude English sports such as cricket and rugby. The GAA played an important part in the fight for independence. This museum, at 82,000-seat Croke Park Stadium in east Dublin, offers a high-tech, interactive introduction to Ireland's favorite games. Relive the greatest moments in hurling and Irish-football history. Then get involved: Pick up a stick and try hurling, kick a football, and test your speed and balance. A 15-minute film (played on request) gives you a "Sunday at the stadium" experience.

Cost and Hours: €6, daily 9:30-17:00, Sun 11:30-17:00, on game Sundays the museum is open to ticket holders only, café, located under the stands at Croke Park Stadium, a 20-minute walk northeast of Parnell Square—enter from St. Joseph's Avenue off Clonliffe Road, tel. 01/819-2323, www.crokepark.ie/gaa-museum.

Tours: The €12, one-hour museum-plus-stadium-tour option is worth it only for rabid fans who want a glimpse of the huge stadium and yearn to know which locker room is considered the unlucky one. The rooftop tour offers views 17 stories above the field from lofty catwalks (€25, daily at 10:30, 11:30, 12:30, 13:30, 14:30, and 15:30).

Hurling or Gaelic Football at Croke Park Stadium

Actually seeing a match here, surrounded by incredibly spirited Irish fans, is a fun experience. Hurling is like airborne hockey with no injury time-outs. Gaelic football resembles a rugged form of soccer; you can carry the ball, but must bounce or kick it every three steps. Matches are held most Saturday or Sunday afternoons in summer (May-Aug), culminating in the hugely popular all-Ireland finals on Sunday afternoons in September. Tickets are available at the stadium except during the finals. Choose a county to support, buy their colors to wear or wave, scream yourself hoarse, and you'll be a temporary local.

Cost and Hours: €15-55, box office open Mon-Fri 9:30-13:00 & 14:15-17:30, www.gaa.ie.

Greyhound Racing

For an interesting, lowbrow look at Dublin life, consider going to the dog races and doing a little gambling. Your best bets are Wednesday, Thursday, and Saturday at Shelbourne Park or Tuesday and Friday at Harold's Cross Racetrack.

Cost and Hours: €10, races start at 20:00, tel. 01/497-1081, www.igb.ie.

DUBLIN

Ireland's Gaelic Athletic Association

The GAA has long been a powerhouse in Ireland. Ireland's national pastimes of Gaelic football and hurling pack stadiums all over the country. When you consider that 80,000 people—paying at least €20 to €30 each—stuff Dublin's Croke Park Stadium and that all the athletes are strictly amateur, you might wonder, "Where does all the money go?"

Ireland has a long tradition of using the revenue generated by these huge events to promote Gaelic athletics and Gaelic cultural events throughout the country in a grassroots and neighborhood way. So, while the players (many of whom are schoolteachers whose jobs allow for evenings and summers free) participate only for the glory of their various counties, the money generated is funding children's leagues, school coaches, small-town athletic facilities, and traditional arts, music, and dance—as well as the building and maintenance of giant stadiums such as Croke Park (which claims to be the third-largest stadium in Europe).

In America, sports are usually considered to be a form of entertainment. But in Ireland, sports have a deeper emotional connection. Gaelic sports are a heartfelt expression of Irish identity. There was a time when the Irish were not allowed to be members of the GAA if they also belonged to a cricket club (a British game).

In 1921, during the War of Independence, Michael Collins (leader of the early IRA, the man who practically invented urban guerrilla warfare) orchestrated the simultaneous assassination of a dozen British intelligence agents around Dublin in a single morning. The same day, the Black and Tans retaliated. These grizzled British WWI veterans, clad in black police coats and tan surplus army pants, had been sent to Ireland to stamp out the rebels. Knowing Croke Park would be full of Irish Nationalists, they entered the packed stadium during a Gaelic football match and fired into the stands, killing 13 spectators as well as a Tipperary player. It was Ireland's first Bloody Sunday, a tragedy that would be repeated 51 years later in Derry.

Today Croke Park's "Hill 16" grandstands are built on rubble dumped here after the 1916 Uprising; it's literally sacred ground. And the Hogan stands are named after the murdered player from Tipperary. Queen Elizabeth II visited the stadium during her historic visit in 2011. Her warm interest in the stadium and in the institution of the GAA did much to heal old wounds.

Shopping in Dublin

Shops are open roughly Monday-Saturday 9:00-18:00 and until 20:00 on Thursday. Hours are shorter on Sunday (if they're open at all). Good shopping areas include:

• **Grafton Street,** with its neighboring streets and arcades (such as the fun Great George's Arcade between Great George's and Drury Streets), and nearby shopping centers (Powerscourt Townhouse and St. Stephen's Green). Francis Street creaks with antiques.

• **Henry Street,** home to Dublin's top department stores (pedestrian-only, off O'Connell Street).

• **Nassau Street,** lining Trinity College, with the popular Kilkenny department store, the Irish Music store, and lots of touristy shops.

• **Temple Bar,** worth a browse any day for its art, jewelry, New Age paraphernalia, books, music (try Claddagh Records), and gift shops. On Saturdays at Temple Bar's Meeting House Square, it's food in the morning (from 9:00) and books in the afternoon (until 18:00).

• **Millennium Walk,** a trendy lane stretching two blocks north from the River Liffey to Abbey Street. It's filled with hip restaurants, shops, and coffee bars. It's easy to miss—look for the south entry at the pedestrian Millennium Bridge, or the north entry at Jervis Street LUAS stop.

• **Street markets,** such as Moore Street (produce, noise, and lots of local color, Mon-Sat 8:00-18:00, closed Sun, near General Post Office), and St. Michan Street (fish, Tue-Sat 7:00-15:00, closed Sun-Mon, behind Four Courts building).

Entertainment in Dublin

Ireland has produced some of the finest writers in the English and Irish languages, and Dublin houses some of Europe's best theaters. Though the city was the site of the first performance of Handel's *Messiah* (1742), these days Dublin is famous for its rock bands: U2, Thin Lizzy, Sinéad O'Connor, and Live Aid founder Bob Geldof's band the Boomtown Rats all started here.

Theater
Abbey Theatre is Ireland's national theater, founded by W. B. Yeats in 1904 to preserve Irish culture during British rule (€15-40, generally nightly at 19:30, Sat matinees at 14:00, 26 Lower Abbey Street, tel. 01/878-7222, www.abbeytheatre.ie). **Gate Theatre** does foreign plays as well as Irish classics (Cavendish Row, tel. 01/874-4045, www.gatetheatre.ie). The **Gaiety Theatre** offers a wide range of quality productions (King Street South, tel. 0818/719-388,

www.gaietytheatre.ie). Street theater takes the stage in Temple Bar on summer evenings. Browse the listings and fliers at the TI.

Concerts
O2 Theatre, once a railway terminus (easy LUAS access), is now sponsored by a hip phone company. Residents call it by its geographic nickname: The Point. It's considered the country's top live-music venue (East Link Bridge, tel. 01/676-6170 or 01/676-6154, www.theO2.ie).

At the **National Concert Hall,** the National Symphony Orchestra performs most Friday evenings (€20-40, off St. Stephen's Green at Earlsfort Terrace, tel. 01/417-0000, www.nch.ie).

The **Steeple Sessions** are traditional Irish music concerts in the Unitarian Church at the southwest corner of St. Stephen's Green. The intimate, candlelit setting has fine acoustics that attract Ireland's best trad musicians for 1.5-hour sessions (€15, May-Sept Tue and Thu at 20:00, 112 St. Stephen's Green West, tel. 01/678-8470, www.steeplesessions.com).

Pub Action
Folk music fills Dublin's pubs, and street entertainers ply their trade in the midst of the party people in Temple Bar and among shoppers

on Grafton Street. The Temple Bar area in particular thrives with music—traditional, jazz, and pop. Although it's pricier than the rest of Dublin, it really is the best place for tourists and locals (who come here to watch the tourists).

Gogarty's Pub has top-notch sessions downstairs daily at 14:00 and upstairs nightly from 21:00 (at corner of Fleet and Anglesea, tel. 01/671-1822). Use this pub as a kickoff for your Temple Bar evening. It's also where the Traditional Irish Musical Pub Crawl starts.

A 10-minute hike up the river west of Temple Bar takes you to a twosome with a local and less-touristy ambience. **The Brazen Head,** which lays claim to being the oldest pub in Dublin, is a hit for an early dinner and late live music (nightly from 21:30), with atmospheric rooms and a courtyard perfect for balmy evenings. They also host "Food, Folk, and Fairies" evenings, which, even at €46, are a great value. You get a hearty four-course meal punctuated between courses by soulful Irish history and fascinating Irish mythology (March-Dec daily 19:00-22:00, Jan-Feb Thu and Sat only; by south end of Father Matthew Bridge, 2 blocks west of Christ Church Cathedral at 20 Bridge Street; pub tel. 01/677-9549, show tel. 01/218-8555, www.irishfolktours.com). **O'Shea's**

Merchant Pub, just across the street, is encrusted in memories of County Kerry football heroes. It's filled with locals taking a break from the grind. There's live traditional music nightly at 21:30 (the front half is a restaurant, the magic is in the back half—enter on Bridge Street, tel. 01/679-3797, www.themerchanttemplebar. com).

At **Palace Bar,** climb upstairs to a cozy room that is a favorite for traditional-music sessions (Thu-Sun at 21:00, east end of Temple Bar, where Fleet Street hits Westmoreland Street at 21 Fleet Street, tel. 01/671-7388, www.thepalacebardublin.com).

Porterhouse has an inviting and varied menu, Dublin's best selection of microbrews, and live music. You won't find Guinness here, just tasty homebrews. Try one of their fun sampler trays. You can check their music schedule online (€12-15 entrées, corner of Essex Street East and Parliament Street, tel. 01/671-5715, www. porterhousebrewco.com).

Pubs at two locations of the **Arlington Hotel** host Irish music and dinner shows. At either place, you'll be entertained by an Irish Rovers-type band singing ballads and a dance troupe scuffing up the floorboards to the delight of tour groups (€34, shows nightly 20:00, dinner reservations required, www.arlingtonhoteltemplebar.com). The Arlington Hotel O'Connell Bridge is north of the River Liffey at 23 Bachelors Walk, just off the north end of O'Connell Bridge (tel. 01/804-9100). The Arlington Hotel Temple Bar is south of the river at the corner of Lord Edward Street and Exchange Street Upper, roughly opposite City Hall (tel. 01/670 8777). Make sure you know at which location you're booking reservations.

Sleeping in Dublin

Dublin is popular, loud, and expensive. Rooms can be tight. Book ahead for weekends any time of year, particularly in summer and during rugby weekends. In summer, occasional big rock concerts can make rooms hard to find. On Sundays in September, fans converge on Dublin from all over the country for the all-Ireland finals in Gaelic football and hurling. Prices are often discounted on weeknights (Mon-Thu) and from November through February. Check for specials on hotel websites.

Big and practical places (both cheap and moderate) are most central near Christ Church Cathedral, on the edge of Temple Bar. For classy, older Dublin accommodations, you'll stay a bit farther out (southeast of St. Stephen's Green). If you're a light sleeper or on a tight budget, get a room in quiet Dun Laoghaire or small-town Howth, where rooms are cheaper. Both spots are an easy 25-minute DART train ride into the city.

Sleep Code

(€1 = about $1.30, country code: 353, area code: 01)
S = Single, **D** = Double/Twin, **T** = Triple, **Q** = Quad, **b** = bath-room, **s** = shower only. Breakfast is included and credit cards are accepted unless otherwise noted.

To help you easily sort through these listings, I've divided the accommodations into three categories, based on the price for a standard double room with bath:

$$$ **Higher Priced**—Most rooms €150 or more.
  $$ **Moderately Priced**—Most rooms between €85-150.
    $ **Lower Priced**—Most rooms €85 or less.

Prices can change without notice; verify the hotel's current rates online or by email. For the best prices, always book direct.

South of the River Liffey
Near Christ Church Cathedral

These hotels cluster near Christ Church Cathedral, a five-minute walk from the best evening scene (at Temple Bar), and 10 minutes from the sightseeing center (Trinity College and Grafton Street). The cheap hostels in this neighborhood have some double rooms. Full Irish breakfasts, which cost €8-10 at the hotels, are cheaper at the many small cafés nearby; try the **Queen of Tarts** or **Chorus Café** (see listings under "Eating in Dublin," later).

$$ Jurys Inn Christ Church, one of three Jurys Inns in downtown Dublin, is central and offers business-class comfort in 182 identical rooms. This no-nonsense, American-style hotel chain has a winning keep-it-simple-and-affordable formula. If ye olde is getting old—and you don't mind big tour groups—this is a good option. Request a room far from the noisy elevator (Db-€79-119 Sun-Thu, €109-149 Fri-Sat, breakfast-€10, book long in advance for weekends, check website for discounts, pay Wi-Fi in lobby, parking-€15/day, Christ Church Place, tel. 01/454-0000, US tel. 800-423-6953, www.jurysinns.com, jurysinnchristchurch@jurysinns.com). The other Jurys Inns, described later, are near Connolly Station and Parnell Square.

$$ Harding Hotel is a hardworking, hardwood place with 55 earth-tone rooms that get stuffy on rare hot days (Sb-€55-80; Db-€70-97 Sun-Thu, €99-149 Fri-Sat; extra bed-€25, breakfast-€9; Rick Steves readers get 10 percent discount in 2014 if booking by email or phone—but not online; on weekends, request a quiet upper-floor room away from the fun-but-noisy ground-floor pub; free Wi-Fi, on Fishamble Street across the street from Christ Church Cathedral, tel. 01/679-6500, www.hardinghotel.ie, info@harding-hotel.ie).

DUBLIN

$ Kinlay House, around the corner from Harding Hotel, is the backpackers' choice—definitely the place to go for cheap beds, a central location, and an all-ages-welcome atmosphere. This huge, red-brick, 19th-century Victorian building has 200 metal, prison-style beds in spartan rooms. There are singles, doubles, and four-to six-bed coed dorms (good for families), as well as a few giant dorms. It fills up most days—call well in advance, especially for singles, doubles, and summer weekends (S-€30-40, Sb-€40-50, D-€50-60, Db-€60-66, T-€72-87, Tb-€87-96, dorm beds-€12-18, includes continental breakfast, guest computer, free Wi-Fi, free 10-minute international phone call, kitchen access, launderette-€8, left luggage-€1/day, travel desk, TV lounge, small lockers-€1/day, lots of stairs, Christ Church, 2-12 Lord Edward Street, tel. 01/679-6644, www.kinlaydublin.ie, info@kinlaydublin.ie).

$ Four Courts Hostel is a 234-bed hostel beautifully located immediately across the river from the Four Courts. It's within a five-minute walk of Christ Church Cathedral and Temple Bar. Bare and institutional (as hostels typically are), it's also spacious and well-run, with a focus on security and efficiency (dorm beds-€12-18, S-€35, Sb-€38-45, bunk D-€40, bunk Db-€45-50, includes small breakfast, elevator, guest computer, free Wi-Fi, free 10-minute international phone call, game room, laundry service, some parking €10/day, left luggage room, 15-17 Merchant's Quay, from Connolly Station or Busáras Central Bus Station take LUAS to Four Courts stop and cross river via Father Matthew Bridge, tel. 01/672-5839, www.fourcourtshostel.com, info@fourcourtshostel.com).

Trinity College Area

You can't get more central than Trinity College; these listings offer a good value for the money.

$$ Trinity Lodge offers fine, quiet lodging in 24 rooms split between two Georgian townhouses on either side of Frederick Street South, just south of Trinity College (Sb-€79-139, Db-€85-159, Tb-€149-209, Qb-€159-250, Wi-Fi, 12 South Frederick Street, tel. 01/617-0900, www.trinitylodge.com, trinitylodge@eircom.net).

$$ Trinity College turns its 800 student-housing rooms on campus into no-frills, affordable accommodations in the city center each summer. Look for the easy-to-miss Accommodations Office (open Mon-Fri 8:00-17:00) inside the huge courtyard, 50 yards down the wall on the left from the main entry arch (late-May-mid-

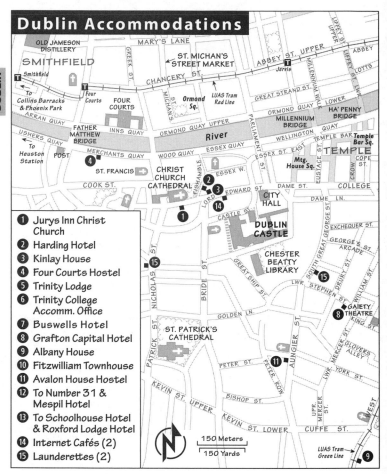

Dublin Accommodations

- ① Jurys Inn Christ Church
- ② Harding Hotel
- ③ Kinlay House
- ④ Four Courts Hostel
- ⑤ Trinity Lodge
- ⑥ Trinity College Accomm. Office
- ⑦ Buswells Hotel
- ⑧ Grafton Capital Hotel
- ⑨ Albany House
- ⑩ Fitzwilliam Townhouse
- ⑪ Avalon House Hostel
- ⑫ To Number 31 & Mespil Hotel
- ⑬ To Schoolhouse Hotel & Roxford Lodge Hotel
- ⑭ Internet Cafés (2)
- ⑮ Launderettes (2)

Sept, S-€58, Sb-€71.50, D-€78, Db-€120, includes continental breakfast, cooked breakfast-€4 extra, tel. 01/896-1177, www.tcd. ie/accommodation/visitors, reservations@tcd.ie).

Near St. Stephen's Green

Dublin is filled with worn-yet-comfy townhouses. Albany House and Fitzwilliam Townhouse are dependable, basic lodgings, while Buswells and Grafton Capital are cushier.

$$ Buswells Hotel, one of the city's oldest, is a pleasant Georgian-style haven with 67 reasonably priced rooms in the heart of the city (Sb-€99-139, Db-€109-159, Tb-€139-169, breakfast-€10, Wi-Fi, between Trinity College and St. Stephen's Green at 23-25 Molesworth Street, tel. 01/614-6500, www.buswells.ie, info@buswells.ie).

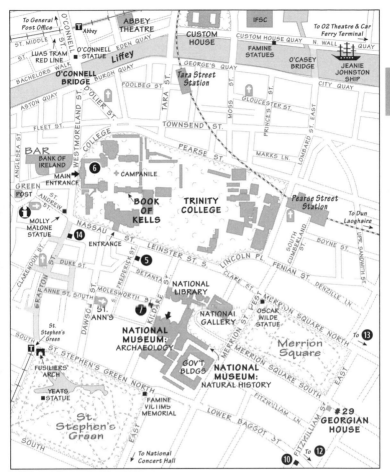

$$ Grafton Capital Hotel has a good central location and 75 rooms. The popular downstairs pub is noisy on weekend nights, so light sleepers should request a room facing the back (Sb-€69-109, Db-€79-129, Tb-€99-159, breakfast-€10, Wi-Fi in lobby, 2 blocks west of St. Stephen's Green on Lower Stephen's Street, tel. 01/648-1100, www.graftoncapitalhotel.com, gm@graftoncapital-hotel.com).

$$ Albany House's 43 restful rooms come with high ceilings, Georgian elegance, and some street noise—request a quieter room at the back (Sb-€60-110, Db-€120-140, Tb-€120-170, Una promises 10 percent off when booking direct by phone or email with this book in 2014, Wi-Fi, just one block south of St. Stephen's Green at 84 Harcourt Street, tel. 01/475-1092, www.albanyhousedublin.com, info@albanyhousedublin.com).

$$ Fitzwilliam Townhouse rents 14 basic rooms in a Georgian townhouse near St. Stephen's Green (Sb-€55-89, Db-€65-115, Tb-€79-125, Qb-€89-135, breakfast-€8-10, free Wi-Fi, 41 Upper Fitzwilliam Street, tel. 01/662-5155, www.fitzwilliamtownhouse. com, info@fitzwilliamtownhouse.com).

$ Avalon House Hostel, near Grafton Street, rents 282 simple, clean backpacker beds in refurbished rooms (dorm beds-€16-22, S-€25-30, Sb-€35, twin D-€50-60, twin Db-€60-70, includes continental breakfast, elevator, guest computer, free Wi-Fi, launderette, kitchen, lockers-€2/day, helpful staff, a few minutes off Grafton Street at 55 Aungier Street, tel. 01/475-0001, www. avalon-house.ie, info@avalon-house.ie).

Away from the Center, Southeast of St. Stephen's Green

The listings that follow are unique places (except for the business-class Mespil Hotel), and they charge accordingly. If you're going to break the bank, do it here.

$$$ Number 31 is a hidden gem reached via gritty little Leeson Close (a lane off Lower Leeson Street). Ask Noel about the VIPs who attended dinner parties here 50 years ago. Its understated elegance is top-notch, with six rooms in a former coach house and 15 rooms in an adjacent Georgian house; the two buildings are connected by a quiet little garden. Guests appreciate the special touches (such as a sunken living room) and tasty breakfasts served in a classy glass atrium (Sb-€110-180, Db-€150-220, Tb-€190-280, Qb-€230-340, Wi-Fi, free parking, 31 Leeson Close, tel. 01/676-5011, www.number31.ie, info@number31.ie).

$$$ The Schoolhouse Hotel taught as many as 300 students in its heyday (1861-1969) and was in the middle of the street fight of the 1916 Easter Uprising. Now it's a serene hideout with 31 pristine rooms and a fine restaurant (Sb-€99-169, Db-€119-199, book early, Wi-Fi, 2-8 Northumberland Road, tel. 01/667-5014, www. schoolhousehotel.com, reservations@schoolhousehotel.com).

$$$ Mespil Hotel is a huge, modern, business-class hotel renting 255 identical three-star rooms (most with a double and single bed, phone, TV) at a good price with all the comforts. This place is a cut above Jurys Inn (Sb, Db, or Tb-€79-195, breakfast-€12, elevator, free Wi-Fi; small first-come, first-served free parking; 10-minute walk southeast of St. Stephen's Green or take bus #37, #38, or #39, 50-60 Mespil Road; tel. 01/488-4600, www. mespilhotel.com, mespil@leehotels.com).

$$ Roxford Lodge Hotel is well-managed and the best value of my Dublin listings. In a quiet residential neighborhood a 25-minute walk from Trinity College, it has 20 tastefully decorated rooms awash with Jacuzzis and saunas. The €150-200 executive suite is honeymoon-worthy (dynamic pricing causes prices to swing high and low—Sb-€55-110, Db-€79-160, Tb-€89-180, Qb-€95-170, best rates online, breakfast-€12, guest computer, free Wi-Fi, secure free parking, 46 Northumberland Road, tel. 01/668-8572, www.roxfordlodge.ie, reservations@roxfordlodge.ie).

North of the River Liffey
Near Connolly Station

This once-tattered neighborhood (like much of the north side) is gradually being rejuvenated.

$$ Jurys Inn Custom House, on Custom House Quay, offers the same value as the other Jurys Inns in Dublin, but it's less central. Its 239 rooms border the financial district, a 10-minute riverside hike from O'Connell Bridge. Of the three Jurys Inns in the city center, this one is more likely to have rooms available (Db-€79-119 Sun-Thu, €109-149 Fri-Sat, breakfast-€10, pay Wi-Fi, parking-€15/day, tel. 01/854-1542, US tel. 800-423-6953, www.jurysinns.com, jurysinncustomhouse@jurysinns.com).

$$ The Townhouse, with 81 small, stylish rooms (some with pleasant views into a central garden courtyard), hides behind a brick Georgian facade one block north of the Customs House (Sb-€49-70, Db-€60-120, Tb-€75-144, guest computer, Wi-Fi, limited parking-€10/day—reserve a spot ahead of time, 47-48 Lower Gardiner Street, tel. 01/878-8808, www.townhouseofdublin.com, info@townhouseofdublin.com).

Near Parnell Square

A swanky neighborhood 250 years ago, this is now workaday Dublin with a steady urban hum.

$$ The Castle Hotel is a formerly grand but still comfortable Georgian establishment embedded in the urban canyons of North Dublin. A half-block east of the Garden of Remembrance, it's a good value with pleasant rooms and the friendly Castle Vaults pub in its basement (Db-€89-129, Tb-€129-149, discounts for 2-night stays, Wi-Fi, Great Denmark Street, tel. 01/874-6949, www.castle-hotel.ie, info@castle-hotel.ie).

$$ Jurys Inn Parnell Street has 253 predictably soulless but good-value rooms. It's a block from the north end of O'Connell Street and the cluster of museums on Parnell Square (Db-€69-119 Sun-Thu, €129-149 Fri-Sat, breakfast-€10, pay Wi-Fi in lobby, tel. 01/878-4900, www.jurysinns.com, jurysinnparnellst@jurysinns.com).

$$ Belvedere Hotel has 92 plain-vanilla rooms that are short on character but long on dependable, modern comforts (Db-€69-99 Sun-Thu, €89-129 Fri-Sat, cheaper if you book online, Wi-Fi,

Great Denmark Street, tel. 01/873-7700, www.belvederehotel.ie, reservations@belvederehotel.ie).

$ Charles Stewart Guesthouse, big and basic, offers 60 forgettable rooms. But it's in a good location for a fair price (Sb-€45-59, Db-€59-79, Tb-€85-119, Qb-€85-139, breakfast-€7, frequent midweek discounts, ask for a quieter room in the back, free Wi-Fi, just beyond top end of O'Connell Street at 5-6 Parnell Square East, tel. 01/878-0350, www.charlesstewart.ie, info@charlesstewart.ie).

Eating in Dublin

It's easy to find fine, creative eateries all over town. While you can get decent pub grub for €12-15 on just about any corner, consider saving that for the countryside. There's just no pressing reason to eat Irish in cosmopolitan Dublin. In fact, going local these days is the same as going ethnic. The city's good restaurants are packed from 20:00 on, especially on weekends. Eating early (17:30-19:00) saves time and money, as many better places offer an early-bird special. Many restaurants serve free jugs of ice water with a smile.

Quick and Easy near Grafton Street

Cornucopia is a small, earth-mama-with-class, proudly vegetarian, self-serve place two blocks off Grafton. It's friendly and youthful, with hearty €12 lunches and €17 dinner specials (Mon-Wed 8:30-21:00, Thu-Sat 8:30-22:30, Sun 12:00-20:30, 19 Wicklow Street, tel. 01/677-7583).

The Farm, Dublin's healthiest dining option, shuns processed food and features fresh, organic, and free-range fare that's affordable and pretty darn tasty (€15-25 main courses, €22 two-course and €25 three-course early-bird specials before 19:00, daily 11:00-22:00, a half-block south of Trinity College at 3 Dawson Street, tel. 01/671-8654).

O'Neill's Pub is a venerable, dark, and tangled retreat offering good grub, including dependable €12-15 carvery lunches. It's very central, located across from the main TI (daily 12:00-22:00, Suffolk Street, tel. 01/679-3656).

Avoca Café is a good-value eatery, with simple yet satisfying meals. It's on the second floor of Avoca department store (€9-17 lunches, Mon-Sat 9:30-17:30, Sun 11:00-17:30, a half-block from the TI at 11-13 Suffolk Street, tel. 01/672-6019).

Two pubs on Duke Street—**The Duke** and **Davy Burns**— serve reliable pub lunches. (The nearby Cathach Rare Books shop, at 10 Duke Street, displays a rare edition of *Ulysses* inscribed by Joyce, among other treasures, in its window.)

Bewley's Café is an old-time favorite, offering light meals from €10 and full meals for €12-17. Sit on the ground floor among Art Deco lamps and windows by stained-glass artist Harry Clarke, or head upstairs to the bright atrium decorated by art students (self-service Mon-Sat 8:00-22:00, Sun 9:00-22:00, 78 Grafton Street, tel. 01/672-7720). For a taste of witty Irish lunch theater, check out **Bewley's Café Theatre** upstairs; you can catch a fun hour-long performance while having a lunch of soup and brown bread for €8-16 (Mon-Sat at 13:00 during a play's run—doors open at 12:45, closed Sun, booking info mobile 086-878-4001, www.bewleyscafetheatre.com).

Wagamama Noodle Bar, like its popular sisters in Britain, is a pan-Asian slurp-a-thon with great and healthy noodle and rice dishes (€12-17) served at long communal tables by energetic waiters (daily 12:00-23:00, often a line but it moves quickly, South King Street underneath St. Stephen's Green Shopping Centre, tel. 01/478-2152).

Yamamori is a plain, mellow, and modern Japanese place serving seas of sushi and noodles (€10-15 lunches daily 12:00-17:30, €16-20 dinners nightly 17:30-23:00, 71 South Great George's Street, tel. 01/475-5001).

Supermarkets: **Dunnes,** on South Great George's Street, is your one-stop shop for assembling a picnic meal (Mon-Sat 8:30-19:00, Thu-Fri until 20:00, Sun 11:00-19:00, across from Yamamori). They have another outlet in the basement of St. Stephen's Green Shopping Centre. **Marks & Spencer** department store has a fancy grocery store in the basement, with fine takeaway sandwiches and salads (Mon-Fri 9:00-20:00, Thu until 21:00, Sat 8:30-20:00, Sun 11:00-19:00, Grafton Street).

Hip and Fun in North Dublin

The Church is a trendy café/bar/restaurant/nightclub/beer garden housed in the former St. Mary's Church. In its former life as a church, it hosted the baptism of Irish rebel Wolfe Tone and the marriage of brewing legend Arthur Guinness. The choir balcony has a huge pipe organ and a refined menu; the ground floor nave is dominated by a long bar and pub grub; and a disco thumps like hell in the bunker-like basement. On warm summer nights, the outdoor terrace is packed. Eating here is as much about the scene as the cuisine (pub grub daily 12:00-20:00, balcony restaurant open daily 17:00-22:30, €24 three-course early-bird special before 19:00, reservations a good idea Fri and Sat nights, corner of St. Mary's and Jervis Streets, tel. 01/828-0102, www.thechurch.ie).

The Epicurean Food Hall offers a fun selection of food stalls with big and splittable portions. Choices include Greek, Mexican, Chinese, Thai, Turkish, Italian, Brazilian, and good old Irish fish-and-chips. It's a hit with locals—and visitors—needing to

DUBLIN

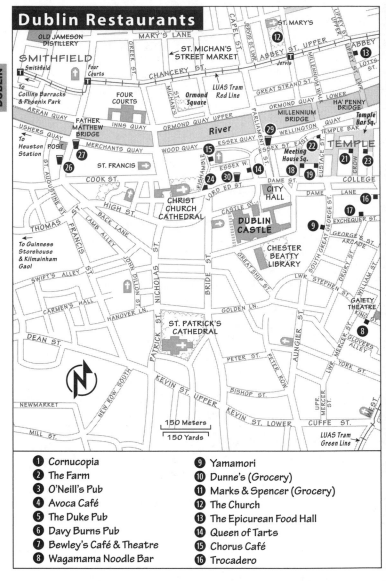

Dublin Restaurants

1. Cornucopia
2. The Farm
3. O'Neill's Pub
4. Avoca Café
5. The Duke Pub
6. Davy Burns Pub
7. Bewley's Café & Theatre
8. Wagamama Noodle Bar
9. Yamamori
10. Dunne's (Grocery)
11. Marks & Spencer (Grocery)
12. The Church
13. The Epicurean Food Hall
14. Queen of Tarts
15. Chorus Café
16. Trocadero

eat cheaply (Sun-Wed 9:00-19:00, Thu-Sat 9:00-20:00, 100 yards north of the Ha' Penny Bridge on Lower Liffey Street).

Fast and Cheap near Christ Church Cathedral

Many of Dublin's late-night grocery stores sell cheap salads, microwaved meat pies, and made-to-order sandwiches (such as **Spar**

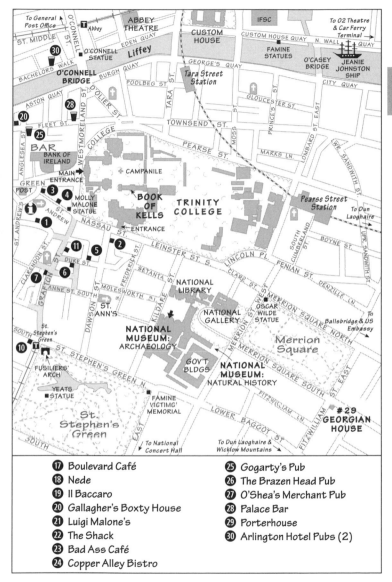

17	Boulevard Café	**25**	Gogarty's Pub
18	Nede	**26**	The Brazen Head Pub
19	Il Baccaro	**27**	O'Shea's Merchant Pub
20	Gallagher's Boxty House	**28**	Palace Bar
21	Luigi Malone's	**29**	Porterhouse
22	The Shack	**30**	Arlington Hotel Pubs (2)
23	Bad Ass Café		
24	Copper Alley Bistro		

and **Centra** markets, open 24 hours a day in the city, spread all over Dublin). A €10 picnic dinner brought back to the hotel might be a good option after a busy day of sightseeing.

Queen of Tarts, with some outdoor seating, does yummy breakfasts, fruit salads, sandwiches, and wonderful pastries. Get yours to go, and enjoy a picnic with a Georgian view in one of

Dublin's grassy squares (€6-8 breakfasts, €8-12 lunches, Mon-Fri 8:00-19:00, Sat-Sun 9:00-19:00, hidden beside Kinlay House on Cow's Lane, tel. 01/670-7499).

Chorus Café is a friendly little hole-in-the-wall diner, perfect for breakfast, lunch, or dinner with a newspaper (€8 breakfasts, €10 lunches, €12-18 dinners, Mon-Fri 8:30-22:00, Sat 9:30-22:00, closed Sun, Fishamble Street, next door to the site of the first performance of Handel's *Messiah*, tel. 01/616-7088).

Dining at Classy Restaurants and Cafés

These stylish restaurants serve well-presented food at fair prices. They're located within a block of each other, just south of Temple Bar and Dame Street, near the main TI.

Trocadero serves beefy European cuisine to Dubliners interested in a slow, romantic meal. The dressy, red-velvet interior is draped with photos of local actors. Come early or make a reservation—it's a favorite with theatergoers (€18-29 meals, Mon-Sat 17:00-24:00, closed Sun, 4 St. Andrew Street, tel. 01/677-5546, www.trocadero.ie). The three-course pre-theater special is a fine value at €25 (17:00-19:00, leave by 19:45).

Boulevard Café is mod, trendy, and likeable, dishing up Mediterranean cuisine that's heavy on the Italian. Their salads, pasta, and sandwiches cost roughly €9-15, and three-course lunch specials are €16 (Mon-Sat 10:00-18:00). It's smart to reserve for dinner, which runs about €17-24 (Mon-Sat 12:00-24:00, closed Sun, 27 Exchequer Street, tel. 01/679-2131, www.boulevardcafe.ie).

In Temple Bar

Il Baccaro, a cozy Italian wine tavern with an arched brick ceiling, is tucked in a quiet corner of Meeting House Square (€15-20 pasta dinners, daily 17:30-22:30, lunches Sat 12:00-16:00 only, closed Sun, tel. 01/671-4597).

Gallagher's Boxty House is touristy and traditional—a good, basic value with creaky floorboards and old Dublin ambience. Its specialty is the boxty, the generally bland-tasting Irish potato pancake filled and rolled with various meats, veggies, and sauces. The "Gaelic Boxty" is the liveliest (€16-23, daily 11:00-22:30, also serves stews and corned beef, 20 Temple Bar, reservations wise, tel. 01/677-2762, http://boxtyhouse.ie).

Luigi Malone's, with its fun atmosphere and varied menu of pizza, ribs, pasta, sandwiches, and fajitas, is just the place to take your high-school date (€15-22 dishes, Mon-Sat 12:00-22:00, Sun 13:00-21:30, corner of Cecilia and Fownes streets, tel. 01/679-2723).

The Shack, while a bit touristy, has a reputation for good quality. It serves traditional Irish, chicken, seafood, and steak dishes (€16-25 entrées, €19 three-course early-bird special offered 17:00-19:00, open daily 12:00-22:00, in the center of Temple Bar, 24 East Essex Street, tel. 01/679-0043).

The Bad Ass Café, where Sinéad O'Connor once waitressed, has been spiffed up since her tenure. The fare is uncomplicated pizza, pasta, burgers, and salads that are cheap by Temple Bar standards. There's even a fun kids menu (€14-19 meals, daily 12:00-22:00, 9-11 Crown Alley, tel. 01/675-3005, live music or comedy most Fri and Sat evenings).

Copper Alley Bistro, a bit farther from the Temple Bar chaos and more reasonably priced, serves comfort-food lunches and dinners (daily 12:00-21:00, corner of Fishamble and Lord Edward streets, just opposite Christ Church Cathedral, tel. 01/679-6500).

Nede may close in 2015. If open, it serves a variety of contemporary Irish dishes inside and on a terrace (€18-27 meals, Mon-Sat 12:30-15:00 & 17:00-22:00, Sun 12:00-16:00 & 18:00-21:30; on Meeting House Square, a half-block off the busy tourist thoroughfare; tel. 01/670-5372).

Dublin Connections

Note that trains and buses generally run less frequently on Sundays. Irish Rail train info: Toll tel. 1850-366-222, www.irishrail.ie.

By Train from Dublin's Heuston Station to: Tralee (every two hours, 6/day on Sun, most change in Mallow but one direct evening train, 4 hours), **Ennis** (7/day, 3.25-3.75 hours, change in Limerick), **Galway** (8/day, 2.5-3 hours).

By Train from Dublin's Connolly Station to: Rosslare (3-4/day, 3 hours), **Portrush** (7/day, 2/day Sun, 5 hours, transfer in Belfast or Coleraine). The **Dublin-Belfast train** connects the two Irish capitals in two hours at 90 mph on one continuous, welded rail (8/day Mon-Sat, 5/day Sun, €40 "day return" tickets, less if you book online, can cost more Fri-Sun). Northern Ireland train info: Tel. 048/9089-9400, www.translink.co.uk.

By Bus to: Belfast (hourly, most via Dublin Airport, 2.75-3 hours), **Trim** (almost hourly, 1 hour), **Ennis** (almost hourly, 4-5.25 hours), **Galway** (hourly, 3.25 hours; faster on CityLink—hourly, 2.5 hours, tel. 890-280-808, www.citylink.ie), **Limerick** (hourly, 2.75-3.25 hours), **Tralee** (7/day, 6 hours), **Dingle** (4/day, 8-9 hours, transfer at Limerick and Tralee). **Bus info:** Tel. 01/836-6111, www.buseireann.ie.

Dublin Airport: The airport is well-connected to the city center seven miles away (airport code: DUB, tel. 01/814-1111, www.dublinairport.ie). To sleep at Dublin Airport, a safe bet is the **$$**

Radisson Blu Dublin Airport (Db-€79-119, best prices if booked online, tel. 01/844-6000, www.radissonblu.ie).

Connecting Ireland and Britain

Spend a few minutes online researching your transportation options across the Irish Sea. Most airline and ferry companies routinely offer discounts for tickets purchased from their websites. And if you have to buy a ferry ticket in person or by phone, you'll be hit with an additional €3 fee. Before sorting out rail/ferry prices with individual companies, try www.arrivatrainswales.co.uk/sail-rail, which deals with several companies and has fares low enough to compete with cheap airlines.

Flights

If you're going directly to London, flying is your best bet. There's no need to waste a valuable day going by slower surface transportation.

Ryanair dominates the discount airline market, but note that its London-bound flights often put in at Luton and Stanstead—airports some distance from the city center (1.5 hours, Irish tel. 1520/444-004, www.ryanair.com). Options to Heathrow include **British Airways** (Irish tel. 1-890-626-747, US tel. 800-247-9297, www.ba.com) and **Aer Lingus** (tel. 081-836-5000, www.aerlingus.com). To get the lowest fares, ask about round-trip ticket prices and book months in advance (though Ryanair offers deals nearly all the time).

Ferries

Discount airlines have cut into ferry business in a big way. But there are still seven daily crossings from Dublin Port (two miles east of O'Connell Bridge) and one daily seasonal crossing from Dun Laoghaire (seven miles south of city center) that all connect to Holyhead, Wales. The route is split between two competing companies; both charge more to take a fast, two-hour crossing (€39) instead of a slower 3.5-hour sailing (€35). Keep in mind that you must board at least 30 minutes before the scheduled sailing time or risk being denied boarding. Since these boats can fill up in advance on summer weekends, try to book at least a week ahead during this peak period.

Dublin to Holyhead: Irish Ferries sails between Dublin Port and Holyhead four times daily, departing at 8:05, 8:45, 14:30, and 20:55 (Dublin tel. 0818-300-400, UK tel. 08705-329-129, www.irish-ferries.com). **Stena Line** sails between Dublin Port and Holyhead three times

daily, departing at 8:20, 15:10, and 21:15 (Dublin tel. 01/204-7777, UK tel. 08447-707-070, www.stenaline.com).

Dun Laoghaire to Holyhead: Stena Line has one daily crossing on a fast, huge catamaran. It leaves April through September only at 13:00 (€42 one-way, 2 hours).

Ferries to France

It makes little sense to waste your valuable time on a 20-hour ferry ride when you can fly to France in three hours. But if the nostalgia of a long, slow ferry ride and the risk of rough seas appeal to you, check **Irish Ferries,** which connects Ireland (Rosslare) with France (Cherbourg and Roscoff) a few days per month from May through September. Cherbourg has the quickest train connection to Paris, but your overall time between Ireland and Paris is about the same (20-hour ferry ride plus 2-hour train trip) regardless of which port is used. One-way fares (€64-84) are cheapest if booked online. In both directions, departures are generally between 15:30 and 17:30 and arrive late the next morning.

While passengers can nearly always get on, reservations are wise in summer and easy online. You can reserve a seat for €15; cabins (2 beds) go for €40-75. The cafeteria serves bad food at reasonable prices. Upon arrival in France, buses and taxis connect you to your Paris-bound train (Irish Ferries: Dublin tel. 0818-300-400, www.irishferries.com).

Dublin Bay

Dangling from opposite ends of Dublin Bay's crescent-shaped shoreline, Dun Laoghaire (dun LEERY) and Howth (rhymes with "growth") are two peas in a pod. They offer quiet, cheap lodging alternatives to Dublin. Both have easy DART light-rail access to the city center, just a 25-minute ride away. Each houses its only worthwhile sightseeing options in pillbox martello (masonry) towers. And they were each once home to a famous Irish writer: James Joyce in Dun Laoghaire and W. B. Yeats in Howth. The fundamental difference between the two is that Dun Laoghaire (south of Dublin) is a ferry port to Wales, while Howth (north of Dublin) is closer to the airport.

Dun Laoghaire

Dun Laoghaire is seven miles south of Dublin. This snoozy suburb, with a ferry terminal for Wales and easy connections to downtown

Dublin, is a convenient small-town base for exploring the big city. But as the majority of ferry crossings have moved to Dublin Port, this town has gotten even quieter in recent years, and it no longer has a TI.

The Dun Laoghaire harbor was strategic enough to merit a line of martello towers, built to defend against an expected Napoleonic invasion (one tower now houses the James Joyce Museum, which may be closed during your visit). By the mid-19th century, its massive breakwaters were completed, protecting a huge harbor. Ships sailed regularly from here to Wales (75 miles away), and the first train line in Ireland connected the terminal with Dublin.

Getting to Dun Laoghaire

Buses run between Dublin and Dun Laoghaire, but the **DART** commuter train is much faster and not subject to Dublin traffic delays (4/hour, 25 minutes, runs Mon-Sat about 6:00-23:30, Sun from 9:00, €2.80 one-way, €5.25 round-trips are good same day only, 3-day pass-€13.90, Eurail Pass valid if you use a counted flexi-day, tel. 01/703-3504, www.irishrail.ie). If you're coming from Dublin, catch a DART train marked *Bray* or *Greystones* and get off at the Sandycove/Glasthule or Dun Laoghaire stop, depending on which

B&B you choose. If you're leaving Dun Laoghaire, catch a train marked *Howth* to get to Dublin. Get off at the central Tara Street Station if you want to sightsee in Dublin, or, for train connections north, ride one stop farther to Connolly Station.

The **Aircoach bus** makes it easy to connect Dublin Airport and Dun Laoghaire. Catch it either at the front steps of the Marine Hotel in Dun Laoghaire or opposite St. Joseph's Church in nearby Glasthule (€9, departs Dun Laoghaire starting at 4:00 and runs from the airport 5:00-23:00, hourly, 50 minutes, tel. 01/844-7118, www.aircoach.ie).

The **taxi** fare from Dun Laoghaire to central Dublin is about €25; to the airport, about €35. With the DART and Aircoach options listed above, taking a taxi is like throwing money away. But if you really need one, try ABC Taxi service (tel. 01/285-5444).

With DART access into Dublin, and cheap or sometimes free parking, Dun Laoghaire is ideal for those with **cars** (which can cost €25/day to park in Dublin).

Orientation to Dun Laoghaire

A busy transportation hub, Dun Laoghaire has a coastline defined by its nearly mile-long breakwaters—reaching like two muscular arms into the Irish Sea. The breakwaters are popular for strollers, bikers, bird-watchers, and fishermen.

Helpful Hints

Internet Access: Central Internet Café provides a fast connection (€4/hour, Mon-Fri 9:00-22:00, Sat 10:00-20:00, Sun 11:00-19:00, 88B Lower George's Street, tel. 01/230-1811).

Post Office: It's on Lower George's Street (Mon-Fri 9:00-18:00, Sat 9:00-13:00, closed Sun).

Laundry: Try **Jeeves,** located in the village of Glasthule, a five-minute downhill walk from Sandycove/Glasthule DART station (€15/load, Mon-Fri 8:30-18:00, Sat 9:00-18:00, closed Sun, full-service only, 34 Glasthule Road, beneath Daniel's Restaurant and Wine Bar, tel. 01/230-1120).

Parking: If you don't have free parking at your B&B, try the pay-and-display street-parking system. Buy a ticket at machines spaced along the street, and display it on your dashboard (Mon-Sat 8:00-19:00, €2/hour, 3-hour max, free Sun).

Best Views: Hike out to the lighthouse, at the end of the East Pier; or climb the tight stairs to the top of the James Joyce Tower and Museum.

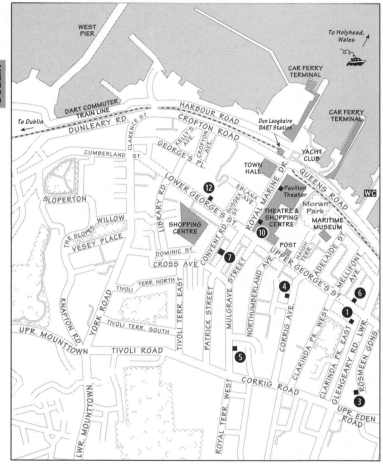

Sights in Dun Laoghaire

James Joyce Tower and Museum

This squat martello tower at Sandycove was originally built to repel a Napoleonic invasion, but it became famous chiefly because of its association with James Joyce. The great author lived here briefly and made it the setting for the opening of his novel *Ulysses*. Unfortunately, the museum, which is run by volunteers, has a history of temporary closures due to funding problems; visitors should call ahead to check its current status. If open, the museum's round exhibition space is filled with literary memorabilia, including photographs and rare first editions. For a fine view, climb the claustrophobic, two-story spiral stairwell sealed inside the thick wall to reach the rooftop gun mount.

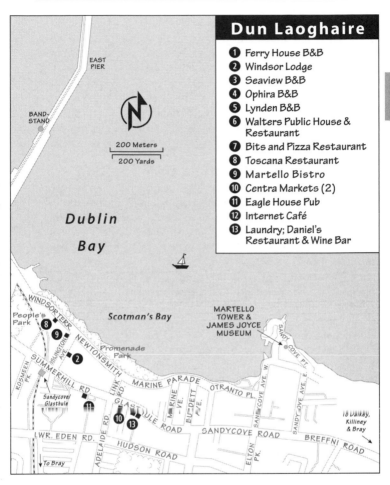

Dun Laoghaire

1. Ferry House B&B
2. Windsor Lodge
3. Seaview B&B
4. Ophira B&B
5. Lynden B&B
6. Walters Public House & Restaurant
7. Bits and Pizza Restaurant
8. Toscana Restaurant
9. Martello Bistro
10. Centra Markets (2)
11. Eagle House Pub
12. Internet Café
13. Laundry; Daniel's Restaurant & Wine Bar

Cost and Hours: Free, March-Oct daily 10:00-18:00, hours may change or museum may be closed in 2014—call ahead or check website to confirm, open by appointment only Nov-Feb, tel. 01/280-9265, www.jamesjoycetower.com.

National Maritime Museum of Ireland

Maritime exhibits fill a former church with model steamships, brass fittings, accounts of heroic rescue attempts, and a huge lighthouse optic (lamp lens, installed where the altar once stood). As earnest as it is, landlubbers may find it underwhelming.

Cost and Hours: €5, daily 11:00-17:00, Haigh Terrace, tel. 01/280-0969, www.mariner.ie.

Plays and Concerts
The Pavilion Theatre offers performances in the center of town (€10-25, box office open Mon-Sat 12:00-17:00, closed Sun, Marine Road, tel. 01/231-2929, www.paviliontheatre.ie).

Swimming
Kids of all ages enjoy swimming at the safe, sandy little cove bordered by rounded rocks beside the martello tower.

Sleeping in Dun Laoghaire

Near Sandycove/Glasthule DART Station
$ Ferry House B&B, with four high-ceilinged rooms, is a family-friendly place on a dead-end street (Sb-€40-50, Db-€65-75, Tb-€90, Qb-€110, €5 discount if you pay cash and book direct, Wi-Fi, 15 Clarinda Park North just off Clarinda Park West, tel. 01/280-8301, www.ferryhousedublin.com, ferry_house@hotmail.com, Eamon and Pauline Teehan).

$ Windsor Lodge rents four fresh, inviting rooms on a quiet street a block off the harbor and a block from the DART station (Db-€50-75, Tb-€70-90, cash only, Wi-Fi, 3 Islington Avenue, tel. 01/284-6952, mobile 086-844-6646, www.windsorlodge.ie, windsorlodgedublin@gmail.com, Mary O'Farrell).

$ Seaview B&B, a modern house run by Mrs. Kane, has three big, cheery rooms and a welcoming guests' lounge with a bright and friendly feeling (S-€30, Db-€60 with this book in 2014, cash only, just above Rosmeen Gardens at 2 Granite Hall, tel. 01/280-9105, www.seaviewbedandbreakfast.com, seaviewbedandbreakfast@hotmail.com).

Near Dun Laoghaire DART Station
$ Ophira B&B is a historic house with four comfortably creaky rooms run by active diver-hiker-biker John O'Connor and his wife Cathy (Sb-€40-55, Db-€60-80, Tb-€75-100, Qb-€120-140, Wi-Fi, parking available, 10 Corrig Avenue, tel. 01/280-0997, www.ophira.ie, johnandcathy@ophira.ie).

$ Lynden B&B, with a classy 150-year-old interior hiding behind a somber front, rents four big rooms (S-€35-40, D-€55-60, Db-€60-70, Wi-Fi, go past Mulgrave Street to 2 Mulgrave Terrace, tel. 01/280-6404, www.lyndenbandb.com, lynden@iol.ie, Maria Gavin).

Eating in Dun Laoghaire

If staying in Dun Laoghaire, I'd definitely eat here rather than in Dublin.

George's Street, Dun Laoghaire's main drag three blocks inland, has plenty of eateries and pubs, many with live music. **Walters Public House and Restaurant** is a bright, modern place above a pub, offering good food to a dressy crowd. The multi-terraced back patio of the pub is great for a drink on a warm evening (€16-24 meals, €8-14 pub meals, daily 15:00-22:00, 68 Upper George's Street, tel. 01/280-7442). A good bet for families is the kid-friendly **Bits and Pizza** (daily 12:00-22:00, off George's Street at 15 Patrick Street, tel. 01/284-2411).

Toscana, on the seafront, is a popular little cubbyhole, serving hearty Italian dishes and pizza. Its location makes it easy to incorporate into your evening stroll. Reserve for dinner (€18 two-course and €21 three-course early-bird specials before 18:30, daily 12:00-22:00, 5 Windsor Terrace, tel. 01/230-0890).

Martello Bistro, also on the stroll-worthy waterfront, is a good bet for seafood or steak in a friendly atmosphere (€23 for two courses, €26 for three courses, Tue-Sun 17:30-22:00, closed Mon, 1 Martello Terrace, tel. 01/280-9871, www.toscana.ie).

Centra Market is centrally located for picnic shopping right on Marine Road (Mon-Sat 7:00-22:00, Sun 8:00-22:00).

Glasthule (called simply "the village" locally, just down the street from the Sandycove/Glasthule DART station) has an array of fun, hardworking little restaurants. The big **Eagle House pub** dishes up hearty €12-20 pub meals in a fun atmosphere; it's a super local joint for a late drink (Mon-Sat 12:00-21:30, Sun 12:00-19:30, 18-19 Glasthule Road, tel. 01/280-4740). The nearby **Daniel's Restaurant and Wine Bar** is less atmospheric, but it's also good (€18-24 meals, Tue-Sun 18:00-22:00, closed Mon, 34 Glasthule Road, tel. 01/284-1027). Another **Centra Market** is right next door and has your picnic makings (daily 7:00-22:00, Glasthule Road).

Howth

Eight miles north of Dublin, Howth rests on a teardrop-shaped peninsula that pokes the Irish Sea. Its active harbor teems with

fishing boats bringing in the daily catch and seals trolling for scraps. Weary Dubliners come here for refreshing coastal cliff walks near the city. Located at the north terminus of the DART light rail line, Howth makes a good place for travelers to settle in, with easy connections to Dublin for sightseeing.

Howth was once an important gateway to Dublin. Near the neck of the peninsula is the suburb of Clontarf, where Irish High

King Brian Boru defeated the last concerted Viking attack in 1014. Eight hundred years later, a squat martello tower was built on a bluff above Howth's harbor to defend it from a Napoleonic invasion that never came. The harbor then grew as a port for shipping from Liverpool and Wales. It was eventually eclipsed by Dun Laoghaire, which was first to gain rail access. Irish rebels smuggled German-supplied guns into Ireland via Howth in 1914, making the 1916 Easter Uprising possible. These days, this is a pleasant, sleepy hamlet.

Getting to Howth

The **DART** light rail system zaps travelers between Howth and the city twice as fast as the bus and sans traffic (4/hour, 25 minutes, runs Mon-Sat about 6:00-23:30, Sun from 9:00, €2.80 one-way, €5.25 round-trips good same day only, 3-day pass-€13.90, Eurail Pass valid if you use a counted flexi-day, tel. 01/703-3504, www.irishrail.ie). If you're coming from Dublin, catch a DART train marked "Howth" (not *Howth Junction, Malahide,* or *Drogheda*) and ride it to the end of the line—passing through Howth Junction en route. All trains departing Howth head straight to Dublin's Connolly Station, and then continue on to Tara and Pearse stations.

If you go by **bus,** #31 or #31B link Dublin's Eden Quay and the well-marked bus stop on Howth's harborfront (1 hour, €2.80). A **taxi** from the airport takes about 20 minutes and costs about €20. Try Executive Cabs (tel. 01/839-6020). With easy DART access into Dublin and plentiful parking, Howth is a good option for those with **cars.**

Orientation to Howth

Howth perches on the north shore of the peninsula, clustered along a quarter-mile harborfront promenade that stretches from the DART station (in the west) to the martello tower on the bluff (in the east). Its two stony piers clutch like crab claws at the Irish Sea. The West Pier has the fishing action and TI, while the East Pier extends to a stubby 200-year-old lighthouse and views of a rugged nearby island, Ireland's Eye. Abbey Street extends south, uphill from the harbor near the base of the martello tower bluff, becoming Main Street with most of the shops and pubs. Along the street, you'll find the post office in the back of the Centra Market (Mon-Fri 9:00-13:00 & 14:15-18:00, Sat 9:00-13:00, closed Sun) and the library (free Internet access, only one terminal, Mon and Wed 14:00-20:30, Tue and Thu-Sat 10:00-13:00 & 14:00-17:00, closed Sun). Ulster Bank has the only ATM in town, across the street from the DART station and to the left of the Gem Market.

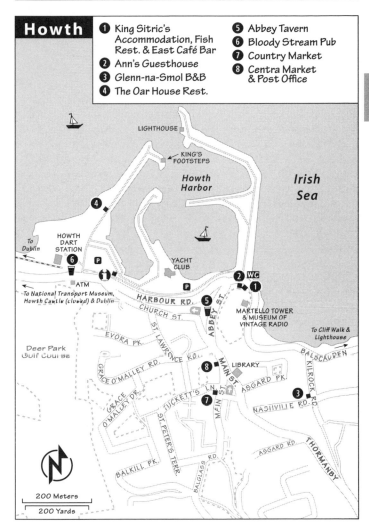

Howth

1 King Sitric's Accommodation, Fish Rest. & East Café Bar
2 Ann's Guesthouse
3 Glenn-na-Smol B&B
4 The Oar House Rest.
5 Abbey Tavern
6 Bloody Stream Pub
7 Country Market
8 Centra Market & Post Office

DUBLIN

Tourist Information

The TI is located on Harbour Road, across from Howth's old courthouse (May-Oct daily 9:00-17:00, shorter hours off-season, tel. 01/839-6955, www.howthismagic.com). If the TI is closed, another good info source is your innkeeper.

Sights in Howth

Other than coastal walks, sightseeing here pales in comparison to Dublin. Nearby Howth Castle is privately owned and cannot be toured.

Museum of Vintage Radio

The three-story martello tower on the bluff overlooking the East Pier is the only sight in Howth worth a glance. Curator Pat Herbert has spent decades acquiring his collection of lovingly preserved radios, phonographs, and even a hurdy-gurdy (a crank-action musical oddity)—all of which still work. Check out the WWII-era radio disguised as a picture frame, which was used by the resistance in occupied France during World War II.

Before leaving the compact bluff, catch the views of the harbor and the nearby island of Ireland's Eye. Spot the distant martello tower on the island's west end and the white guano coating its eastern side, courtesy of a colony of gannets.

Cost and Hours: €5, May-Oct daily 11:00-16:00, Nov-April Sat-Sun 11:00-16:00, entry up driveway off Abbey Street, mobile 086-815-4189.

National Transport Museum

Housed in a large shed on the castle grounds, this is a dusty waste of time unless you find rapture in old trams and buses.

Cost and Hours: €3.50, June-Aug Sat-Sun 14:00-17:00, otherwise by appointment only, tel. 01/848-0831, www.nationaltransportmuseum.org.

St. Mary's Abbey

Looming above Abbey Street, the current ruins date from the early 1400s. Before that, a church built by Norse King Sitric in 1042 stood at this site. The entrance to the ruins is on Church Street, above the abbey grounds.

East and West Piers

The piers make for mellow strolls after a meal. Poke your head into the various fishmonger shops along the West Pier to see the day's catch. At the end of the pier (on the leeward side), you'll find the footsteps of King George IV carved into the stone after his 1821 visit. The East Pier is a quiet jetty barbed with a squat lighthouse  and the closest views of Ireland's Eye. If you want to get even closer to the island, book a boat excursion (€15 round-trip, daily in summer on demand 10:00-18:00, call for off-season trips, mobile 086-845-9154, www.islandferries.net).

Hiking Trails

Trails above the eastern cliffs of the peninsula offer enjoyable, breezy exercise. For a scenic three-hour round-trip, walk past the

East Pier and martello tower, following Balscadden Road uphill. You'll soon pass Balscadden House, where writer W. B. Yeats spent part of his youth (watch for plaque on left). Where the road dead-ends, you'll find the well-marked trailhead. The trail is easy to follow, and soon you'll be walking south around the craggy coastline to grand views of the Bailey Lighthouse on the southeast rim of the peninsula. The gate to the lighthouse grounds is always locked, so enjoy the view from afar before retracing your steps back to Howth.

DUBLIN

Sleeping in Howth

$$$ King Sitric's Accommodation is Howth's best lodging option and has a fine harborfront seafood restaurant (described later). It fills the old harbormaster's house with eight well-kept rooms and a friendly staff (Sb-€110-145, Db-€120-205, Tb-€190-245, discounts for 2-night stay with dinner, online deals, Wi-Fi, East Pier below martello tower, tel. 01/832-5235, www.kingsitric.ie, info@kingsitric.ie, Aidan and Joan MacManus).

$ Ann's Guesthouse, next door to King Sitric's, sports four bright, airy rooms on its top floor—two with skylight views of the harbor (Sb/Db-€80, 5 East Pier, tel. 01/832-3197, jonathancooke.cooke@gmail.com).

$ Glenn-na-Smol B&B is a homey house with six unpretentious rooms in a quiet setting, a 15-minute walk uphill along the coast behind the martello tower (Sb-€40, Db-€70, Tb-€90, Qb-€100, cash only, Wi-Fi, parking, corner of Nashville Road & Kilrock Road, tel. 01/832-2936, mobile 085-716-1695, rickards@indigo.ie, Sean and Kitty Rickard).

Eating in Howth

King Sitric's Fish Restaurant, one of the area's most famous seafood experiences, serves Irish versions of French classics in a dining room (upstairs) with harbor views. Chef Aidan MacManus rises early each morning to select the best of the day's catch on the pier, to be enjoyed that evening by happy customers (€22-30 meals, Mon and Wed-Sat 18:30-22:00, Sun 13:00-19:00, closed Tue, reservations a good idea, tel. 01/832-5235, www.kingsitric.ie). They also operate the more economical **East Café Bar,** on the ground floor with extra seating out front. Their soups, salads, steak sandwiches, and fish dishes are a good value (Wed-Mon 12:30-21:30, closed Tue).

The Oar House sits halfway down the West Pier, serving a variety of great €16-24 fish dishes in a bustling atmosphere (Mon-Sat 12:30-22:00, Sun 12:30-21:00, 8 West Pier, tel. 01/839-4568).

For pub grub, try the **Abbey Tavern** up the hill on Abbey Street (occasional trad music and dance, call for schedule, tel. 01/839-0307 or 01/832-2006). Another good choice is the **Bloody Stream Pub** in front of the DART station (tel. 01/839-5076). The **Country Market** sells picnic supplies, and its cheap and friendly upstairs tea room offers lunch (Mon-Sat 7:00-19:00, Sun 7:00-17:00, Main Street). The **Centra Market** is a block closer to the waterfront (Mon-Fri 6:30-22:00, Sat-Sun 7:00-22:00, Main Street).

NEAR DUBLIN

Valley of the Boyne • Trim • Glendalough • Wicklow Mountains • Irish National Stud

Not far from urban Dublin, the stony skeletons of evocative ruins sprout from the lush Irish countryside. The story of Irish history is told by ancient burial mounds, early Christian monastic settlements, huge Norman castles, and pampered estate gardens. In gentler inland terrain, the Irish love of equestrian sport is nurtured in grassy pastures ruled by spirited thoroughbreds. These sights are separated into three regions: north of Dublin (the Valley of the Boyne, including Brú na Bóinne and the town of Trim), south of Dublin (Powerscourt Gardens, Glendalough, and the Wicklow Mountains), and west of Dublin (the Irish National Stud).

Valley of the Boyne

The peaceful, green Valley of the Boyne, just 30 miles north of Dublin, has an impressive concentration of historical and spiritual sights: The enigmatic burial mounds at Brú na Bóinne are older than the Egyptian pyramids. At the Hill of Tara (seat of the high kings of Celtic Ireland), St. Patrick preached his most persuasive sermon. The valley also contains the first monastery in Ireland built in the style used on the Continent, and several of the country's finest high crosses. You'll see Trim's 13th-century castle—Ireland's biggest—built by Norman invaders, and you can wander the site of the historic Battle of the Boyne (1690), in which the Protestants turned the tide against the Catholics and imposed British rule until the 20th century.

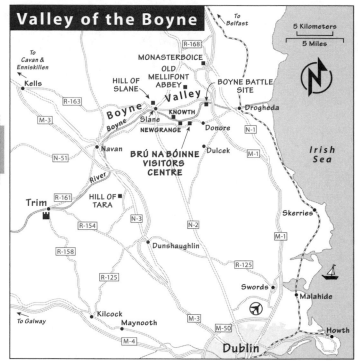

Valley of the Boyne

NEAR DUBLIN

Planning Your Time

Of these sights, only Brú na Bóinne is worth ▲▲▲ (and deserves a good three hours). The others, while relatively meager physically, are powerfully evocative to anyone interested in Irish history and culture. Without a car, I'd visit only Brú na Bóinne, taking the shuttle bus from Dublin.

The region is a joy by car, because all of the described sights are within a 30-minute drive of one another. If you eat your Weet-abix and get an early start, you could see the entire region in a day. Though the sights are on tiny roads, they're well-marked with brown, tourist-friendly road signs. You'll navigate best using an Ordnance Survey atlas.

As you plan your Ireland itinerary, if you're flying into or out of Dublin but want to avoid the intensity and expense of that big city, consider using Trim as an overnight base (45-minute drive from airport) and tour these North of Dublin sights from there.

Tours of the Valley of the Boyne

If you lack a car and like tours, consider a round-trip excursion from Dublin. **Mary Gibbon's Tours** visits Brú na Bóinne (including inside the Newgrange tomb), the Hill of Tara, and the Hill of Slane in a seven-hour trip (€35, Mon-Fri only, 9:30 pickup at Mespil Hotel at 50-60 Mespil Road, 10:15 pickup at Dublin TI on Suffolk Street, 10:25 pickup at AIB Bank at 37-38 Upper O'Connell Street, home by 16:30, book direct rather than through TI, mobile 086-355-1355, www.newgrangetours.com, info@newgrangetours.com).

Brú na Bóinne

The famous archaeological site of Brú na Bóinne—"dwelling place of the Boyne"—is also commonly called "Newgrange," after its star attraction. Here you can visit two ▲▲▲, 5,000-year-old passage tombs—**Newgrange** and **Knowth** (rhymes with "south"). These are massive grass-covered burial mounds built atop a hill, with a chamber inside reached by a narrow stone passage. Mysterious, thought-provoking, and mind-bogglingly old, these tombs can give you chills.

Planning Your Visit: There are three sights to see at Brú na Bóinne: Newgrange, Knowth, and the state-of-the-art visitors center with its excellent museum. You start at the visitors center—no one is allowed to visit the tombs on their own. From here, you buy your ticket and catch the next available shuttle bus to the tombs, where a guide gives a 30-minute tour.

Each tomb site takes about 1.5 hours to visit (30-minute round-trip bus ride plus 30-minute guided tour plus 30 minutes of free time). The museum at the visitors center is well worth an additional 30-60 minutes. If you add in waiting time for the next available shuttle bus, you're looking at a minimum of 2.5 hours to do one of the tombs (along with the museum), or 4 hours to do both tombs (and museum).

Which tomb is best? If you can't see both, I'd pick Newgrange because it's more famous and allows you inside. (On the other hand, wait times for the Newgrange shuttle bus can be longer.) Knowth is bigger and more impressive on the outside, but you can't go in. Each site is different enough and worthwhile, but for many, seeing just one is adequate. You might pick your tomb according to whichever shuttle bus is leaving next.

Orientation to Brú na Bóinne

Cost: Newgrange-€6, Knowth-€5; the museum is included in both tomb prices.

Hours: May-Sept daily 9:00-18:30, slightly shorter hours off-season, last entry to visitors center 45 minutes before closing. Newgrange is open year-round, while Knowth is open Easter to mid-Oct only.

Crowd-Beating Tips: Arrive early—ideally before 10:00 in peak season—to avoid the big midday bus-tour crowds from Dublin. Visits are limited, and on busy summer days those arriving in the afternoon may not get a spot on a shuttle bus. No reservations are possible, and the last bus to the tombs leaves 1.75 hours before closing.

Getting There: By **car,** drive 45 minutes north from Dublin on N-1 to Drogheda, where signs direct you to the visitors center. If you're using a GPS, input "Brú na Bóinne" rather than "Newgrange" to get to the visitors center, where you must check in.

Without a car, you could take Mary Gibbon's **tour,** which includes the passage tombs (see "Tours of the Valley of the Boyne," earlier).

Or take the **Newgrange shuttle bus,** a 15-seat van that runs daily from Dublin to the visitors center. It departs Dublin at 8:45 and 11:15 from Gresham Hotel on Upper O'Connell Street, and at 9:00 and 11:30 from the Dublin TI on Suffolk Street. Return trips depart Brú na Bóinne at 13:30 and 16:30. Since it generally fills up in summer (and may not run every day in winter), seat reservations are essential. Depending on your departure time, you'll have 3.5 to 6.5 hours of sightseeing time; keep in mind it's logistically tricky (though not impossible) to see both tombs in 3.5 hours (€17 round-trip, 45 minutes each way, must book in advance, run by Over the Top Tours, tel. 01/838-6128 or Ireland toll-free 1-800-424-252, www.overthetoptours.com).

Information: Tel. 041/988-0300, www.heritageireland.ie.

Visiting Brú na Bóinne

Brú na Bóinne Visitors Center and Museum

Buy your ticket (to one or both tombs), find out when the next shuttle bus leaves, then spend your waiting time in the excellent museum, grabbing lunch in the cheery cafeteria, and using the WCs (they're scarce at the tomb sites).

The museum introduces you to the Boyne River Valley and its tombs. No one knows who built the 40 burial mounds found in the surrounding hills. Exhibits re-create what these pre-Celtic people might have been like—simple farmers and hunters living in huts, fishing in the Boyne, equipped with crude tools of stone, bone, or wood.

Then around 3200 B.C., someone had a bold idea. They constructed a chamber of large stones, with a long stone-lined passage leading up to it. They covered it with a huge mound of dirt and rocks in successive layers. Sailing down the Boyne to the sea, they beached at Clogherhead (12.5 miles from here), where they found hundreds of five-ton stones, weathered smooth by the tides. Somehow they transported them back up the Boyne, possibly by tying a raft to the top of the stone so it was lifted free by a high tide. They then hauled these stones up the hill by rolling them over logs and up dirt ramps, and laid them around the perimeter of the burial mound to hold everything in place. It would have taken anywhere from five years to a generation to construct a single large tomb.

Why build these vast structures? Presumably, it was to bury VIPs. A dead king might be carried up the hill to be cremated on a pyre. Then they'd bring his ashes into the tomb, parading by torchlight down the passage to the central chamber. The remains were placed in a ceremonial basin, mingled with those of his illustrious ancestors.

To help bring the history to life, the museum displays replicas of tools and objects found at the sites, including the ceremonial basin stone and a head made out of flint, which may have been carried atop a pole during the funeral procession. Marvel at the craftsmanship of the perfectly spherical stones (and the phallic one), and wonder at their purpose.

The tombs may also have served an astronomical purpose; they're precisely aligned to the movements of the sun, as displays and a video illustrate. You can request a short tour and winter solstice light-show demo at a full-size replica of the Newgrange passage and interior chamber.

Since the tombs are aligned with the heavens, it begs the question: Were these structures sacred places where primal Homo sapiens gathered to ponder the deepest mysteries of existence?

Newgrange

This grassy mound atop a hill is 250 feet across and 40 feet high. Dating from 3200 B.C., it's 500 years older than the pyramids at Giza. The base of the mound is ringed by dozens of "kerbstones," each about nine feet long and weighing five tons.

The entrance facade is a mosaic of white quartz and dark granite. This is a reconstruction done in the 1970s, and not every archaeologist agrees it originally looked like this. Above the doorway is a square window called the roofbox, which played a key role (as we'll see). In front of the doorway lies the most famous of the kerbstones, the 10- by 4-foot entrance stone. Its left half is carved with three mysterious spirals, which have become a kind of poster child for prehistoric art.

Most of Newgrange's kerbstones have designs carved into them. This was done with super-hard flint tools; the Neolithic ("New Stone Age") people had not mastered metal. The stones feature common Neolithic motifs: not people or animals, but geometric shapes—spirals, crosshatches, bull's-eyes, and chevrons.

Entering the tomb, you walk down a narrow 60-foot passage lined with big boulders. Occasionally you have to duck or turn sideways to squeeze through. The passage opens up into a central room—a cross-shaped central chamber with three alcoves, topped by a 20-foot-high igloo-type stone dome. Bones and ashes were placed here in a ceremonial stone basin, under 200,000 tons of stone and dirt.

While we know nothing of Newgrange's builders, it most certainly was a sacred spot—for a cult of the dead, a cult of the sun, or both. The tomb is aligned precisely east-west. As the sun rises on the shortest day of the year (winter solstice, Dec 21), a ray of light enters through the roofbox and creeps slowly down the passageway. For 17 minutes, it lights the center of the sacred chamber (your guide will demonstrate this). Perhaps this was the moment when the souls of the dead were transported to the afterlife, via that ray of life-giving and life-taking light. Then the light passes on, and, for the next 364 days, the tomb sits again in total darkness.

Knowth

This site is an impressive necropolis, with one grand hill-topping mound (similar to Newgrange) surrounded by several smaller satellite tombs. The central mound is 220 feet wide, 40 feet high, and covers 1.5 acres.

You'll see plenty of mysteriously carved kerbstones and new-feeling grassy mounds that you can look down on from atop the grand tomb.

Knowth's big tomb has two passages: one entering from the east, and one from the west. Like Newgrange, it's likely aligned so the rising and setting sun shone down the passageways to light the two interior chambers. Neither passage is open to the public, but you can visit a room carved into the mound by archaeologists, where a cutaway lets you see the layers of dirt and rock used to build the mound. You also get a glimpse down one of the passages.

The Knowth site thrived from 3000 to 2000 B.C. The central tomb dates from about 2000 B.C. It was likely used for burial rituals and sun-tracking ceremonies to please the gods and ensure the regular progression of seasons for crops. The site then evolved into the domain of fairies and myths for the next 2,000 years, and became an Iron Age fortress in the early centuries after Christ. Around A.D. 1000, it was an all-Ireland political center, and later, a Norman fortress was built atop the mound. Now, 4,000 years after prehistoric people built these strange tombs, you can stand atop the hill at Knowth, look out over the surrounding countryside, and contemplate.

More Sights in the Valley of the Boyne

▲▲Battle of the Boyne Site

One of Europe's lesser-known battlegrounds (but huge in Irish and British history), this is the pastoral riverside site of the pivotal bat-

tle in which the Protestant British broke Catholic resistance, establishing Protestant rule over all Ireland and Britain.

Cost and Hours: €4, daily May-Sept 10:00-18:00, March-April 9:30-17:30, Oct-Feb 9:00-17:00, last admission one hour before closing, tearoom/cafeteria, tel. 041/980-9950, www.battleoftheboyne.ie.

Background: It was here in 1690 that Protestant King William III, with his English/Irish/Dutch/Danish/French Huguenot army, defeated his father-in-law—who was also his uncle—Catholic

King James II and his Irish/French army. King William's forces, on the north side of the Boyne, managed to fight their way across the river, and by the end of the day, King James was fleeing south in full retreat. He soon left Ireland, but his forces fought on until their final defeat a year later. James the Second (called "James da Turd" by those who scorn his lack of courage and leadership) never returned, and he died a bitter ex-monarch in France. King William of Orange's victory, on the other hand, is still celebrated in Northern Ireland every July 12, with controversial marches by Unionist "Orangemen."

The 50,000 soldiers who fought here made this the largest battle ever to take place in the British Isles. Yet it was only a side skirmish in an even larger continental confrontation pitting France's King Louis XIV against the "Grand Alliance" of nations threatened by France's dominant military and frequent incursions into neighboring lands.

Louis ruled by divine right, answerable only to God—and James modeled himself after Louis. Even the pope (who could control neither Louis nor James and was equally disturbed by Catholic France's aggressions) backed Protestant King William against

Catholic King James—just one example of the pretzel logic that was the European mindset at the time.

The site of the Battle of the Boyne was bought in 1997 by the Irish Office of Public Works, part of the Republic's governmental efforts to respect a place sacred to Unionists in Northern Ireland—despite the fact that the battle's outcome ensured Catholic subordination to the Protestant minority for the next 230 years.

Visiting the Site: The **Visitors Centre** is housed in a mansion built on the battlefield 50 years after the conflict. The exhibits do a good job illustrating the international nature of the battle and its place in the wider context of European political power struggles. The highlight is a huge battleground model with laser lights that move troops around the terrain, showing the battle's ebb and flow on that bloody day. A separate 15-minute film (shown in the former stable house) runs continuously and does a fine job of fleshing out the battle.

The Sunday afternoon **"Living History" demonstrations** (June-Aug) are a treat for history buffs and photographers, with guides clad in 17th-century garb. You'll get a bang out of the musket loading and firing demo (at 11:00, 13:00, 15:00, and 17:00), see cavalry combat in full gallop (at 12:00, 14:00, and 16:00), and learn that to be an Irish watermelon is to fear the sword.

▲Hill of Tara

This site was the most important center of political and religious power in pre-Christian Ireland. While aerial views show plenty of mystifying circles and lines, wandering with the sheep among the well-worn ditches and hills leaves you with more to feel than to see. Visits are made meaningful by an excellent 20-minute video presentation and the caring 20-minute guided walk that follows (available upon request and entirely worthwhile). Wear good walking shoes—the ground is uneven and often wet.

Cost and Hours: €3, includes video and guided walk, June-mid-Sept daily 10:00-18:00, last tour at 17:00; during off-season access is free but visitors center is closed; tel. 046/902-5903.

Visiting the Site: You'll see the Mound of Hostages (a Bronze Age passage grave, c. 2500 B.C.), a couple of ancient sacred stones, a war memorial, and vast views over the Emerald Isle. While ancient Ireland was a pig pile of minor chieftain-kings scrambling for power, the high king of Tara was king of the mountain. It was at this ancient stockade that St. Patrick directly challenged the king's authority. When confronted by the high king, Patrick convincingly explained the Holy Trinity using a shamrock: three petals with one stem. He won the right to preach Christianity throughout Ireland, and the country had a new national symbol.

This now-desolate hill was also the scene of great modern

events. In 1798, passionate young Irish rebels chose Tara for its defensible position, but were routed by better organized (and more sober) British troops. (The cunning British commander had sent three cartloads of whiskey along the nearby road earlier in the day, knowing the rebels would intercept it.) In 1843, the great orator and champion of Irish liberty Daniel O'Connell gathered 500,000 Irish peasants on this hill for his greatest "monster meeting"—a peaceful show of force demanding the repeal of the Act of Union with Britain (kind of the Woodstock of its day). In a bizarre final twist, a small group of British Israelites—who believed they were one of the lost tribes of Israel, who had ended up in Britain—spent 1899 to 1901 recklessly digging up parts of the hill in a misguided search for the Ark of the Covenant.

Stand on the Hill of Tara. Think of the history it's seen, and survey Ireland. It's understandable why this "meeting place of heroes" continues to hold a powerful place in the Irish psyche.

Old Mellifont Abbey

This Cistercian abbey (the first in Ireland) was established by French monks who came to the country in 1142 to bring the Irish monks more in line with Rome. (Even the abbey's architecture was unusual, marking the first time in Ireland that a formal, European-style monastic layout was used.) Cistercians lived isolated rural lives; lay monks worked the land, allowing the more educated monks to devote all their energy to prayer. After Henry VIII dissolved the abbey in 1539, centuries of locals used it as a handy quarry. Consequently, little survives beyond the octagonal lavabo, where the monks would ceremonially wash their hands before entering the refectory to eat. The lavabo gives a sense of the abbey's former grandeur.

The excellent 45-minute tours, available upon request and included in your admission, give meaning to what you're seeing. To get a better idea of the extent of the site, be sure to check out the model of the monastery in its heyday, located at the back of the small museum next to the ticket desk.

Cost and Hours: €3, mid-May-mid-Sept daily 10:00-17:00, last tour at 16:30, last entry 45 minutes before closing, no tours mid-Sept-mid-May when site is free and you can explore on your own, tel. 041/982-6459, www.heritageireland.ie.

Monasterboice

This ruined monastery is visit-worthy for its round tower and its ornately carved high crosses—two of the best such crosses in Ireland. In the Dark Ages, these crosses, illustrated from top to bottom with Bible stories, gave monks a teaching tool as they preached to the illiterate masses. Imagine the crosses in their prime, when they were brightly painted (before years of wind and rain weathered the paint away). Today, Monasterboice is basically an old graveyard.

Cost and Hours: Free and always open.

Visiting the Site: The 18-foot-tall **Cross of Murdock** (Muiredach's Cross, c. 923, named after an abbot) is considered the best high cross in Ireland. The circle—which characterizes the Irish high cross—could represent the perfection of God. Or, to help ease pagans into Christianity, it may represent the sun, which was worshipped in pre-Christian Celtic society. Whatever its symbolic purpose, its practical function was to support the weight of the crossbeam.

Face the cross (with the round tower in the background) and study the carved sandstone. The center panel shows the Last

Judgment, with Christ under a dove, symbolizing the Holy Spirit. Those going to heaven are on Christ's right, and the damned are being ushered away by a pitchfork-wielding devil on his left. Working down, you'll see the Archangel Michael weighing souls, as the Devil tugs demonically at the scales; the adoration of the three—or four—Magi; Moses striking the rock to bring forth water; scenes from the life of David; and, finally, Adam, Eve, and the apple next to Cain slaying Abel. Imagine these carvings with their original, colorful paint jobs. Check out the plaque at the base of the nearby tree, which further explains the carvings on the cross.

Find the even taller cross nearest the tower. It seems the top section was broken off and buried for a period, which protected it from weathering. The bottom part remained standing, enduring the erosive effect of Irish weather, which smeared the once-crisp features.

The door to the round tower was originally 15-20 feet above the ground (accessible by ladder). After centuries of burials, the ground level has risen.

Trim

The sleepy, workaday town of Trim, straddling the River Boyne, is marked by the towering ruins of Trim Castle. Trim feels littered with mighty ruins that seem to say, "This little town was big-time...750 years ago." The tall Yellow Steeple (over the river from the castle) is all that remains of the 14th-century Augustinian Abbey of St. Mary. Not far away, the Sheep's Gate is a humble remnant of the once-grand medieval town walls. Near the town center, the modest, 30-foot-tall Wellington Column honors native son Arthur Wellesley, the First Duke of Wellington (1769-1852), who spent his childhood in Trim, defeated Napoleon at Waterloo, and twice became prime minister.

Trim makes a great landing pad into—or launching pad out of—Ireland. If you're flying into or out of Dublin Airport and don't want to deal with big-city Dublin, this is a perfect alternative— an easy 45-minute, 30-mile drive away. You can rent a car at the airport and make Trim your first overnight base (getting used to driving on the other side of the road in easier country traffic). Or spend your last night here before returning your car at the airport. Weather permitting, my evening stroll (described later) makes for a fine first or last night in the Emerald Isle.

Orientation to Trim

Trim's main square is a traffic roundabout, and everything's within a block or two. Most of the shops and eateries are on or near Market Street, along with banks and a supermarket.

Tourist Information
The TI is right next to the castle entrance and includes a handy coffee shop. Drop in to pick up a free map and check out the collage of photos in the entryway, showing the castle dolled up for the filming of *Braveheart* (June-Aug Mon-Fri 9:30-17:30, Sat-Sun 12:00-17:30, shorter hours Sept-May, Castle Street, tel. 046/943-7227).

The TI organizes historical walking tours of the town, led by enthusiastic volunteers (€5, pay at TI, daily at 14:30 and 19:00, one hour; tours depart from the bog oak sculpture—facing the TI, go 100 feet down sidewalk to right; tel. 046/943-7227).

Helpful Hints
Internet Access: The **library** offers 30 minutes of free Internet access (Tue and Thu 10:00-20:30, Wed and Fri-Sat 10:00-13:00 & 14:00-17:00, closed Sun-Mon, High Street).

Post Office: It's tucked in the back of the **Spar Market** (Mon-Fri 9:00-17:30, Sat 9:00-13:00, closed Sun, Emmett Street).

Laundry: The launderette is located close to Market Street (€10/ load, Mon-Sat 9:00-13:00 & 14:00-17:30, closed Sun, Watergate Street, tel. 046/943-7176).

Parking: To park on the street or in a public lot, use the pay-and-display parking system. Buy a ticket at one of the machines spaced along the street, and display it on your dashboard (€1/ hour, 2-hour max, Mon-Sat 9:00-18:00, free Sun).

NEAR DUBLIN

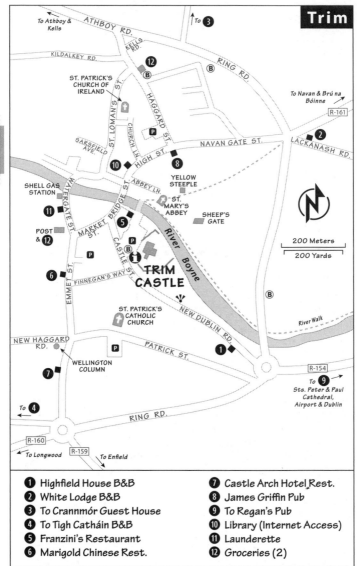

❶ Highfield House B&B	❼ Castle Arch Hotel Rest.
❷ White Lodge B&B	❽ James Griffin Pub
❸ To Crannmór Guest House	❾ To Regan's Pub
❹ To Tigh Catháin B&B	❿ Library (Internet Access)
❺ Franzini's Restaurant	⓫ Launderette
❻ Marigold Chinese Rest.	⓬ Groceries (2)

Taxi: DKs Taxi can give you a lift to nearby Boyne sites (tel. 085/132-3005).

Fishing Tours: Marc O'Regan leads backcountry trout and pike fishing trips, making a splash with anglers who want to experience Ireland's bountiful lakes and rivers (tel. 046/943-1635, www.crannmor.com). O'Regan and his wife also run the recommended Crannmór Guest House.

Sights in Trim

▲▲Trim Castle

This is the biggest Norman castle in Ireland. Set in a grassy riverside park at the edge of this sleepy town, its mighty keep towers above a very ruined outer wall. It replaced a wooden fortification that was destroyed in 1173 by Irish High King Rory O'Connor, who led a raid against the invading Normans. The current castle was completed in the 1220s and served as a powerful Norman statement to the restless Irish natives. It remained a sharp barb at the fringe of "the Pale" (English-controlled territory), when English rule shrank to just the area around Dublin in the 1400s. By that time, any lands farther west were "beyond the Pale."

Cost and Hours: €3 for castle grounds, €4 for entrance to keep and required tour; roughly April-Oct daily 10:00-18:00; Nov-March Sat-Sun 10:00-17:00, closed Mon-Fri; last entry one hour before closing, 45-minute tours run 2/hour but spots are limited and can fill up—so arrive early in peak season, tel. 046/943-8619, www.heritageireland.ie.

Visiting the Castle: Today the castle remains an impressive sight—so impressive that it was used in the 1994 filming of *Braveheart* (which was actually about Scotland's—not Ireland's—fight for freedom from the English). The best-preserved walls ring the castle's southern perimeter and sport a barbican gate that contained two drawbridges.

At the base of the castle walls, notice the cleverly angled "batter" wall—used by defenders who hurled down stones that banked off at great velocity into the attacking army. Notice also that the castle is built directly on bedrock, visible along the base of the walls. During sieges, while defenders of other castles feared that attackers would tunnel underground to weaken the defensive walls, that was not an issue here.

The massive 70-foot-high central keep, which is mostly a hollow shell, has 20 sides. This experimental design was not implemented elsewhere because it increased the number of defenders needed to cover all the angles. You can go inside the keep only with the included tour, where you'll start by checking out the cool ground-floor models showing the evolution of the castle. Then you'll climb a series of tightly winding original staircases and modern, high catwalks, learn about life in the castle, and end at the top with great views of the walls and the countryside.

Make time to take a 15-minute walk outside, circling the castle walls and stopping at the informative plaques that show the castle from each viewpoint during its gory glory days. Night strollers are treated to views of the castle hauntingly lit in blue-green hues.

Trim Evening Stroll

Given good weather, here's my blueprint for a fine night in Trim. Start the evening by taking the pleasant **River Walk** stroll along the River Boyne from Trim Castle. Cross the wooden footbridge over the river behind the castle and turn right (east). The paved, level trail leads under a modern bridge and extends a mile along fields that serfs farmed 750 years ago. During the filming of *Braveheart*, Mel Gibson's character met the French princess in her tent in these fields, with the castle looming in the background.

The trail ends in the medieval ruins of **Newtown.** This was indeed once the "new town" (mid-1200s) that sprouted as a religious satellite community to support political power housed in the castle. Wander the sprawling, ragtag ruins of **Saints Peter and Paul Cathedral** (1206), once the largest Gothic church in Ireland.

Just beyond the ruins, cross the old Norman bridge to the 13th-century scraps of the **Hospital of St. John the Baptist.** Medieval medicine couldn't have been fun, but this hospital was the best you could hope for back when life was nasty, brutish, and short. Many a knight was spent here.

Cross back over the bridge and stop for a pint at tiny, atmospheric **Regan's,** one of the oldest pubs in Ireland, set beside one of the oldest bridges in Ireland. Drink a toast to Rock Hudson, who filmed a pivotal scene from *Captain Lightfoot* (1955) on the bridge.

Then walk back along the river the way you came and have dinner at the recommended **Franzini's** restaurant beside the castle. After dinner, assist your digestion by walking a lap around the castle (beautifully lit up at night). End the evening a few blocks away with a pint at the **James Griffin** pub (described later). A fine night 'tis...or 'twas.

The Power & Glory

This grade-schoolish, 30-minute slideshow overview of the personalities and history of the castle is followed by an exhibit on life here in Norman times. The show and a cup of coffee help to pass the time as you wait for your castle tour.

Cost and Hours: €3, Mon-Sat 9:30-17:30, Sun 12:00-17:00, shorter hours off-season, show runs on demand, in visitors center with TI next to castle, Castle Street, tel. 046/943-7227.

Sleep Code

(€1 = about $1.30, country code: 353, area code: 046)
S = Single, **D** = Double/Twin, **T** = Triple, **Q** = Quad, **b** = bathroom, **s** = shower only. Credit cards are accepted and breakfast is included unless otherwise noted.

To help you easily sort through these listings, I've divided the accommodations into two categories, based on the price for a standard double room with bath:

$$ Higher Priced—Most rooms more than €70.
$ Lower Priced—Most rooms €70 or less.

Prices can change without notice; verify the hotel's current rates online or by email. For the best prices, always book direct.

Sleeping in Trim

$$ Highfield House B&B, across the street from the castle and a five-minute walk from town, is a stately 185-year-old former maternity hospital, with hardwood floors and nine spacious, high-ceilinged rooms (Sb-€50-55, Db-€78-84, Tb-€99-110, family-friendly, guest computer, Wi-Fi; overlooks roundabout where Dublin Road hits Trim, just before castle at Castle Street; tel. 046/943-6386, www.highfieldguesthouse.com, info@highfieldguesthouse.com, Geraldine and Edward Duignan).

$ White Lodge B&B, a 10-minute walk northwest of the castle, has six comfortably unpretentious rooms with an oak-and-granite lounge (Sb-€45, Db-€70, Tb-€81, Qb-€94, 10 percent discount for active-duty members of the US and Canadian armed forces with this book, guest computer, Wi-Fi, parking, New Road, tel. 046/943-6549, www.whitelodgetrim.com, whitelodgetrim@eircom.net, Todd O'Loughlin). They also offer a family-friendly self-catering house next door. A handy 300-yard trail leads from across the street to the castle (enter next to the modern sculptures).

Countryside B&Bs
These two B&Bs are in the quiet countryside about a mile outside Trim (phone ahead for driving directions).

$$ At **Crannmór Guest House,** north of town, Anne O'Regan decorates five rooms with cheery color schemes (Sb-€45-55, Db-€76-80, Tb-€90, Qb-€110, Wi-Fi, Dunderry Road, tel. 046/943-1635, mobile 087-288-7390, www.crannmor.com, cranmor@eircom.net). Her professional-guide husband Marc knows all the best fishing holes.

$$ Mrs. Keane's **Tigh Catháin B&B,** southwest of town, has four large, bright, lacy rooms with a comfy, rural feel and organically grown produce at breakfast (Db-€70-75, Tb-€85-95, cash only, Wi-Fi, on R160/Longwood Road, tel. 046/943-1996, mobile 086-257-7313, www.tighcathain-bnb.com, tighcathain.bnb@ gmail.com).

Eating in Trim

A country-market town, Trim offers basic meat-and-potatoes lunch and dinner options. Don't waste time searching here for gourmet food. The restaurants and cafés along Market Street are friendly, wholesome, and unassuming (soup-and-sandwich delis close at 17:30).

Franzini's is the only place in town with a fun dinner menu and enough business to make it work. They serve pasta, steak, fish, and good salads in a modern, candlelit ambience. Nothing's Irish except the waiters (€15-24 dishes, €20 two-course or €25 three-course early-bird dinners before 19:30, Mon-Sat 17:00-22:00, Sun 13:00-21:00, French's Lane across from the castle parking lot, tel. 046/943-1002).

Marigold fits the bill if you're in the mood for Chinese food (Mon-Sat 17:00-23:00, Sun 16:00-23:00, Emmett Street, tel. 046/943-8788).

The **Castle Arch Hotel,** popular with locals, serves hearty pub grub at reasonable prices in its bistro (€11-14 meals, daily 12:30-21:30, tel. 046/943-1516).

For a fun pub experience, check out Trim's two best watering holes. The **James Griffin** (on High Street) is full of local characters and old-fashioned atmosphere, with traditional Irish music sessions on Monday and Wednesday nights. Tiny, low-ceilinged **Regan's** is a fun, unpretentious pub next to the old Norman bridge over the River Boyne. You'll find it at the north end of the bridge, a half-mile stroll outside of town next to the ruins of Newtown.

Supermarkets: **Spar Market** has everything you need to create a picnic (daily 8:00-21:00, Emmett Street). The same goes for **Super Valu,** a larger store on Haggard Street that's a bit farther from the town center (daily 8:00-22:00).

Trim Connections

Trim has no train station; the nearest is in Drogheda 25 miles away on the coast. Buses from Trim to **Dublin** (almost hourly, 1 hour) pick you up at the bus shelter next to the TI and castle entrance on Castle Street. For details, see www.buseireann.ie.

Glendalough and the Wicklow Mountains

The Wicklow Mountains, while only 15 miles south of Dublin, feel remote—enough so to have provided a handy refuge for opponents to English rule. Rebels who took part in the 1798 Irish uprising hid out here for years. When the frustrated British built a military road in 1800 to help flush out the rebels, the area became more accessible. Today, this same road—now R-115—takes you through the Wicklow area to Glendalough at its south end. While the valley is the darling of the Dublin day-trip tour organizers, it doesn't live up to the hype. But two blockbuster sights—Glendalough and the Gardens of Powerscourt—make a visit worth considering.

NEAR DUBLIN

Getting Around

By car or tour, it's easy. If you lack wheels, take a tour. It's not worth the trouble on public transport.

By Car: It's a delight. Take N-11 south from Dublin toward Bray, then R-117 to Enniskerry, the gateway to the Wicklow Mountains. Signs direct you to the gardens and on to Glendalough. From Glendalough, if you're heading west, you can leave the valley (and pick up the highway to the west) over the famous but dull mountain pass called the Wicklow Gap.

By Tour from Dublin: Wild Wicklow Tours covers the region with an entertaining guide who packs every minute with information and *craic* (interesting, fun conversation). With a gang of 40 packed into tight but comfortable, mountain-gripping buses, the guide kicks into gear from the first pickup in Dublin. Tours cover Dublin's embassy row, Dun Laoghaire, the Bay of Dublin (with the mansions of Ireland's rich and famous), the windy military road over scenic Sally Gap, and the Glendalough monasteries (€28, €25 for students and readers with this book in 2014, daily year-round, 9:10 pickup at Dublin TI on Suffolk Street, 10:00 pickup at Dun Laoghaire ferry terminal, stop for lunch at a pub—cost not included, return through Dun Laoghaire and on to Dublin by 17:30, Dun Laoghaire-ites could stay on the bus to continue into Dublin for the evening, advance booking required, tel. 01/280-1899, www.wildwicklow.ie).

Over the Top Tours bypasses mansions and gardens to focus on Wicklow rural scenery. Stops include Glendalough, Sally Gap, the Glenmacnass waterfall, and Blessington lakes (€28, 9:20 pickup at Gresham Hotel on Upper O'Connell Street, 9:45 pickup at

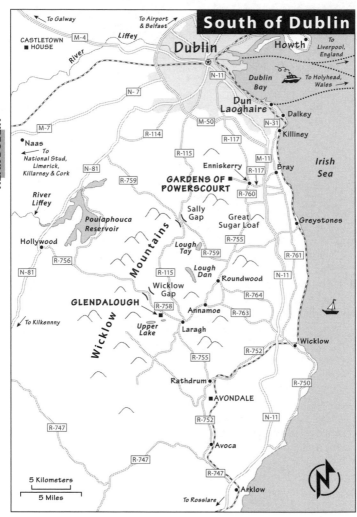

Dublin TI on Suffolk Street, return by 17:30, 14-seat minibus, reservations required, hold seat by leaving credit-card number, Ireland toll-free tel. 1-800-424-252, Dublin tel. 01/860-0404, mobile 087-259-3467, www.overthetoptours.com, info@overthetoptours.com).

Sights in the Wicklow Area

▲▲Gardens of Powerscourt

A mile above the village of Enniskerry, the Gardens of Powerscourt cover several thousand acres within the 16,000-acre estate. The dreamy driveway alone is a mile long. While the mansion's in-

terior, only partially restored after a 1974 fire, isn't much, its meticulously kept aristocratic gardens are Ireland's best. The house was commissioned in the 1730s by Richard Wingfield, first viscount of Powerscourt. The gardens, created during the Victorian era (1858-1875), are called "the grand finale of Europe's formal gardening tradition...probably the last garden of its size and quality ever to be created." I'll buy that.

NEAR DUBLIN

Upon entry, you'll get a flier laying out 40-minute and one-hour walks. The "one-hour" walk takes 30 minutes at a slow amble. With the impressive summit of the Great Sugar Loaf Mountain as a backdrop, and a fine Japanese garden, Italian garden, and goofy pet cemetery along the way, this attraction provides the scenic greenery I hoped to find in the rest of the Wicklow area. The lush movies *Barry Lyndon* and *The Count of Monte Cristo* were filmed in this well-watered aristocratic fantasy.

Spend five minutes checking out the easy-to-miss "To Have and To Hold" room, which provides a history of the estate and model of Powerscourt House before the fire.

Cost and Hours: €8.50, daily 9:30-17:30, last entry at 17:00, great cafeteria, tel. 01/204-6000, www.powerscourt.ie.

Nearby: Skip the Powerscourt Waterfall (€5.50, 4 miles/6.5 km away). Kids may enjoy a peek at the antique dollhouses of the upstairs Museum of Childhood (€3, Mon-Sat 10:00-17:00, Sun 12:00-17:00).

Sleeping in Enniskerry: Drivers coming straight from Dublin Airport can stay overnight in Enniskerry at **$$ Brook Cottage B&B,** a quiet guesthouse that's popular with hikers. It has a rambling floor plan and sports six rooms, comfortable beds, and traditional breakfasts in a country setting (Sb-€50-55, Db-€80, Tb-€100-105, Qb-€100-110, cash only, 10 percent discount for multiple-night stays, Wi-Fi, tel. 01/276-6039, mobile 086-824-1687, www.enniskerry.org, brookcottagebb@eircom.net, Mary Moran). From the Enniskerry clock tower, go 1.8 miles (3 km) up Kilgarron Hill toward Glencree, look for the last bus stop on the left (with a big bus turn-around on the right followed by the B&B sign on the right), turn left (directly across from the B&B sign) down a narrow lane (Shop River Road), and pass through the green gates.

▲Military Road over Sally Gap

This trip is only for those with a car. From the Gardens of Powerscourt and Enniskerry, go to Glencree, where you drive the tiny military road over Sally Gap and through the best scenery of the Wicklow Mountains (on Sundays, watch for dozens of bicycle racers). Look for the German military cemetery, built for U-boat sailors who washed ashore in World War II. Near Sally Gap, notice the peat bogs and the freshly cut peat bricks drying in the wind. Many locals are nostalgic for the "good old days," when homes were always peat-fire heated. At the Sally Gap junction, turn left, where a road winds through the vast Guinness estate. Look down on the glacial lake (Lough Tay) and the Guinness mansion (famous for jet-set parties). Nicknamed "Guinness Lake," the water looks like Ireland's favorite dark-brown stout, and the sand of the beach actually looks like the head of a Guinness beer. From here, the road meanders scenically down into the village of Roundwood and on to Glendalough.

▲▲Glendalough

The steep wooded slopes of Glendalough (GLEN-da-lock, "Valley of the Two Lakes"), at the south end of Wicklow's military road, hide Ireland's most impressive monastic settlement. Founded by St. Kevin in the sixth century, the monastery flourished (despite repeated Viking raids) throughout the Age of Saints and Scholars until the English destroyed it in 1398. Though it was finally abandoned during the Dissolution of the Monasteries in 1539, pilgrims kept coming, especially on St. Kevin's Day, June 3. (This might have something to do with the fact that a pope said seven visits to Glendalough had the same indulgence—or forgiveness from sins—value as one visit to Rome.) While much restoration was done in the 1870s, most of the buildings date from the 10th-12th century.

The valley sights are split between the two lakes. The lower lake has the visitors center and the best buildings. The upper lake has scant ruins and feels like a state park, with a grassy lakeside picnic area and school groups. Walkers and hikers will enjoy a choice of nine different trails of varying lengths through the lush Wicklow countryside (longest loop takes four hours, hiking-trail maps available at visitors center).

Planning Your Time: Park for free at the Glendalough Visitors Centre. Visit the center, wander the ruins (free) around the round tower, walk the traffic-free Green Road one mile to the upper lake, and then walk back to your car. Or you can drive to the upper lake (more free parking—except July-Aug, when it's €4). If you're rushed, skip the upper lake. Summer tour-bus crowds are terrible all day on weekends and 11:00-14:00 on weekdays.

Cost and Hours: Visitors center-€3, daily mid-March-mid-Oct 9:30-18:00, mid-Oct-mid-March 9:30-17:00, last entry 45 minutes before closing, tel. 0404/45352.

Visiting Glendalough: Start out at the **Glendalough Visitor**

Centre, where a 20-minute video provides a good thumbnail background on monastic society in medieval Ireland. While the video is more general than specific to Glendalough, the adjacent museum room does feature this particular monastic settlement. The model in the center of the room re-creates the fortified village of the year 1050. A browse through the interactive exhibits here shows the contribution these monks made to intellectual life in Dark Age Europe (such as illuminated manuscripts and Irish minuscule, a more compact alphabet developed in the seventh century).

From the visitors center, a short and scenic walk along the Green Road takes you to the round tower of the **monastic village.**

Easily the best ruins of Glendalough gather around this famous 110-foot-tall round tower. Towers like this (usually 60-110 feet tall) were standard features in such settlements, functioning as bell towers, storage lofts, beacons for pilgrims, and last-resort refuges during Viking raids (though given enough warning, monks were safer hiding in the surrounding forest). The towers had a high door with a pull-up ladder—both for safety and because a door at ground level would have weakened the tower's foundation. Several ruined churches (10th-12th century) and a sea of grave markers complete this evocative scene. Markers give short descriptions of the ruined buildings.

In an Ireland without cities, these monastic communities were mainstays of civilization. They were remote outposts where ascetics (with a taste for scenic settings) gathered to commune with God. In the 12th century, with the arrival of grander monastic orders such as the Franciscans and the Dominicans and with the growth of cities, these monastic communities were eclipsed. Today, Ireland is dotted with the reminders of this age: illuminated manuscripts, simple churches, carved crosses, and about 100 round towers.

The Green Road continues one mile farther up the valley to the **Upper Lake.** The oldest ruins—scant and hard to find—lie near this lake. If you want a scenic Wicklow walk, begin here.

▲Avondale House

Located in south County Wicklow (known as the Garden County), this mansion is the birthplace and lifelong home of Charles Stewart Parnell, the Nationalist politician and dynamo often called the "uncrowned King of Ireland."

Upon entering the opulent Georgian "big house" (built in 1777), you'll first view an informative 20-minute video on Parnell's life. Then you're set free to roam with a handout outlining each room's highlights. A fine portrait of Parnell graces the grand, high-ceilinged entry hall, and a painting of his American grandfather, who manned the USS *Constitution* in the War of 1812, hangs in one room. The dining room is all class, with fine plasterwork and hardwood floors. Original furniture such as Parnell's sturdy canopied bed graces the remaining rooms, and many come with cozy fireplaces and views. The lush surrounding estate of over 500 acres, laced with pleasant walking trails, was used by the Irish Forestry Service (Coillte) to try out forestry methods.

Cost and Hours: €7; June-Aug daily 11:00-17:00; Sept-Oct Tue-Sun 11:00-16:00, closed Mon; shorter hours off-season; café, tel. 0404/46111, www.coillte.ie.

Getting There: It's best to visit by car, as Avondale House is too far for the Dublin day-tour buses (45 miles south of Dublin). Trains depart Dublin's Connolly station (4/day, 1.5 hours) to Rathdrum; Avondale is a short taxi ride away (1.5 miles south of town).

Irish National Stud

Ireland's famed County Kildare—just west of Dublin—has long been known to offer the perfect conditions for breeding horses. Its reputation dates all the way back to the 1300s, when Norman war horses were bred here. Kildare's grasslands lie on a bedrock table of limestone, infusing the soil with just the right mix of nutrients for grazing horses. And the nearby River Tully sparkles with high levels of calcium carbonate, essential for building strong bones in the expensive thoroughbreds (some owned by Arab sheikhs) raised and raced here.

In 1900, Colonel William Hall-Walker (Scottish heir to the Johnny Walker distilling fortune) bought a farm on the River Tully and began breeding a line of champion thoroughbreds. His amazing successes and bizarre methods were the talk of the sport. In 1916, the colonel donated his land and horse farm to the British government, which continued breeding horses here. The farm was eventually handed over to the Irish government, which in 1945 created the Irish National Stud Company to promote the thoroughbred industry.

Today, a tour of the grounds at the Irish National Stud gives you a fuller appreciation for the amazing horses that call this place home. Animal lovers and horse-racing fans driving between Dublin and Galway can enjoy a couple of hours here, combining the tour with lunch (inside the decent cafeteria or at a picnic table by the parking lot) and a stroll through the gardens.

Orientation to the Irish National Stud

Cost: €12.50 includes guided tour of the Irish National Stud, plus entry to Japanese Gardens, St. Fiachra's Garden, and Horse Museum.

Hours: Daily Feb-Oct 9:30-18:00, Nov 9:30-17:00, closed Dec-Jan, last entry one hour before closing, 30-minute tours run 3/day at 12:00, 14:30, and 16:00, tel. 045/522-963, www.irish-national-stud.ie.

Getting There: From M-7, **drivers** take exit #13 and follow the signs five minutes south (don't take exit #12 for the Curragh Racecourse). **Trains** departing Dublin's Heuston Station stop at Kildare town (1-3/hour, 45 minutes, www.irishrail.ie). A shuttle bus runs from Kildare's train station to the National Stud (2/hour), or you can take a taxi (about €12-15). One **bus** departs Dublin's Busáras Station Monday through Saturday at 9:30 and returns from the National Stud at 15:45. On Sunday, two buses run, departing Busáras at 10:00 and 12:00, with returns at 15:00 and 17:30. Confirm this schedule at the bus station in Dublin.

Visiting the Irish National Stud

The guided tour begins in the **Sun Chariot Yard** (named for the winner of the 1942 Fillies Triple Crown), surrounded by stables housing pregnant mares. A 15-minute film of a foal's birth runs continuously in a stall in the corner of the yard.

The adjacent **Foaling Unit** is where births take place, usually from February through May. The gestation period for horses is 11 months, with 90 percent of foals born at night. (In the wild, a mare and her foal born during the day would have been vulnerable to predators as the herd moved on. Instead, horses have adapted so that foals are born at night—and are able to keep up with the herd within a few hours.) Eccentric Colonel Hall-Walker noted the position of the moon and stars at the time of each foal's birth, and sold those born under inauspicious astrological signs (regardless of their parents' stellar racing records).

From here, you'll pass a working saddle-making shop and a forge where horseshoes are still hammered out on an anvil.

At the **Stallion Boxes,** you'll learn how stargazing Colonel Hall-Walker installed skylights in the stables—allowing the heavens maximum influence over the destiny of his prized animals. A brass plaque on the door of each stall proudly states the horse's name and its racing credentials. One stall bears the simple word, "Teaser." The unlucky occupant's job is to identify mares in heat...

When Irish Horses Are Running

Every Irish town seems to have a betting shop for passionate locals who love to closely follow (and wager on) their favorite horses. A quick glance at the weekend sports sections of any Irish newspaper gives you an idea of this sport's high profile. Towns from Galway to Dingle host annual horse races that draw rabid fans from all over.

The five most prestigious Irish races take place at the **Curragh Racecourse,** just south of Kildare town (March-Oct, 1 hour west of Dublin, 10 minutes from the National Stud, www.curragh.ie). Horses have been raced here since 1741. The broad, open fields nearby are where the battle scenes in *Braveheart* were filmed (the neighboring Irish army base provided the blue-face-painted extras).

but rarely is the frustrated stallion given the opportunity to breed. Bummer.

After the tour, meander down the pleasant tree-lined **Tully Walk,** with paddocks on each side. You'll see mares and foals running free, with the occasional cow thrown in for good measure (cattle have a calming effect on rowdy horses). To ensure you come home with all your fingers, take full note of the *Horses Bite and Kick* signs. These superstar animals are bred for high spirits—and are far too feisty to pet.

Other Sights: Visitors with extra time can explore three more attractions (all included in your entry ticket). The tranquil and photogenic **Japanese Gardens** were created by the colonel to depict the trials of life (beware the Tunnel of Ignorance). A wander through the more extensive and natural **St. Fiachra's Garden** (the patron saint of gardening) demands more time. Equestrian buffs may want to linger among the memorabilia in the small **Horse Museum,** where you can get a grip on how many hands it takes to measure a horse.

PRACTICALITIES

This section covers just the basics on traveling in the Republic of Ireland (for much more information, see *Rick Steves' Ireland*). You can find free advice on specific topics at www.ricksteves.com/tips.

Money

Ireland uses the euro currency: 1 euro (€) = about $1.30. To convert prices in euros to dollars, add about 30 percent: €20 = about $26, €50 = about $65. (Check www.oanda.com for the latest exchange rates.)

The standard way for travelers to get euros is to withdraw money from ATMs (which locals may call "cash points") using a debit card, ideally with a Visa or MasterCard logo. Before departing, call your bank or credit-card company: Confirm that your card will work overseas, ask about international transaction fees, and alert them that you'll be making withdrawals in Europe. Also ask for the PIN number for your credit card in case it'll help you use Europe's "chip-and-PIN" payment machines (see below); allow time for your bank to mail your PIN to you. To keep your valuables safe, wear a money belt.

Dealing with "Chip and PIN": Much of Europe—including Ireland—is adopting a "chip-and-PIN" system for credit cards, and some merchants rely on it exclusively. European chip-and-PIN cards are embedded with an electronic chip, in addition to the magnetic stripe used on our American-style cards. This means that your credit (and debit) card might not work at payment machines, such as those at train and subway stations, toll roads, parking garages, luggage lockers, and self-serve gas pumps. Memorizing your credit card's PIN lets you use it at some chip-and-PIN machines—just enter your PIN when prompted. If a payment machine won't take your card, look for a machine that takes cash or see if there's a cashier nearby who can process your transaction. Often the easiest solution is to pay for your purchases with cash you've withdrawn from an ATM using your debit card (Europe's ATMs still accept magnetic-stripe cards).

Phoning

Smart travelers use the telephone to reserve or reconfirm rooms, reserve restaurants, get directions, research transportation connections, confirm tour times, phone home, and lots more.

To call Ireland from the US or Canada: Dial 011-353 and then the area code (minus its initial zero) and local number. (The 011 is our international access code, and 353 is Ireland's country code.)

To call Ireland from a European country: Dial 00-353 followed by the area code (minus its initial zero) and local number. (The 00 is Europe's international access code.)

To call within Ireland: If you're dialing within an area code, just dial the local number; but if you're calling outside your area code, you have to dial both the area code (which starts with a 0) and the local number.

To call from Ireland to another country: Dial 00 followed by the country code (for example, 1 for the US or Canada), then the area code and number. If you're calling European countries whose phone numbers begin with 0, you'll usually have to omit that 0 when you dial.

Tips on Phoning: A mobile phone—whether an American one that works in Ireland, or a European one you buy when you arrive—is handy, but can be pricey. If traveling with a smartphone, switch off data-roaming until you have free Wi-Fi. With Wi-Fi, you can use your smartphone to make free or inexpensive domestic and international calls by taking advantage of a calling app such as Skype or FaceTime.

To make cheap international calls from any phone (even your hotel-room phone), you can buy an international phone card. These work with a scratch-to-reveal PIN code, allow you to call home to the US for pennies a minute, and also work for domestic calls.

Another option is buying an insertable phone card. These are usable only at pay phones, are reasonable for making calls within the country, and work for international calls as well (though not as cheaply as the international phone cards). But be aware that phone booths are becoming scarcer in Ireland, and those that remain are often out of order. Note that insertable phone cards—and most international phone cards—work only in the country where you buy them.

Calling from your hotel-room phone is usually expensive,

From:	rick@ricksteves.com
Sent:	Today
To:	info@hotelcentral.com
Subject:	Reservation request for 19-22 July

Dear Hotel Central,

I would like to reserve a room for 2 people for 3 nights, arriving 19 July and departing 22 July. If possible, I would like a quiet room with a double bed and a bathroom inside the room.

Please let me know if you have a room available and the price.

Thank you!
Rick Steves

unless you use an international phone card. For much more on phoning, see www.ricksteves.com/phoning.

Making Hotel and B&B Reservations

To ensure the best value, I recommend reserving rooms in advance, particularly during peak season. Email the hotelier or B&B host with the following key pieces of information: number and type of rooms; number of nights; date of arrival; date of departure; and any special requests. (For a sample form, see the sidebar.) Use the European style for writing dates: day/month/year. For example, for a two-night stay in July, you could request: "1 double room for 2 nights, arrive 16/07/14, depart 18/07/14." Hoteliers typically ask for your credit-card number as a deposit.

Know the terminology: An "en suite" room has a bathroom (toilet and shower/tub) actually inside the room; a room with a "private bathroom" can mean that the bathroom is all yours, but it's across the hall. A "standard" room could have two meanings. Big hotels sometimes call a basic en-suite room a "standard" room to differentiate it from a fancier "superior" or "deluxe" room. At small hotels and B&Bs, guests in a "standard" room have access to a bathroom that's shared with other rooms and down the hall.

Given the economic downturn, hoteliers may be willing to make a deal—try emailing several hotels to ask for their best price. In general, hotel prices can soften if you do any of the following: stay in a "standard" room, offer to pay cash, stay at least three nights, or travel off-season.

Eating

The traditional "Irish Fry" breakfast includes juice, tea or coffee, cereal, eggs, bacon, sausage, toast, a grilled tomato, sautéed mushrooms, and black pudding. If it's too much for you, just order the items you want.

To dine affordably at classier restaurants, look for "early-bird specials" (offered about 17:30–19:00, last order by 19:00). At a sit-down place with table service, tip about 10 percent—unless the service charge is already listed on the bill.

Smart travelers use pubs (short for "public houses") to eat, drink, and make new friends. Pub grub is Ireland's best eating value. For about $15–20, you'll get a basic hot lunch or dinner. The menu is hearty and traditional: stews, soups, fish-and-chips, meat, cabbage, potatoes, and—in coastal areas—fresh seafood. Order drinks and meals at the bar. Pay as you order, and don't tip.

When you say "a beer, please" in an Irish pub, you'll get a pint of Guinness. (If you think you don't like Guinness, try it in Ireland.) For a cold, refreshing, basic, American-style beer, ask for a lager, such as Harp. If you want a small beer, ask for a glass or a half-pint.

Craic (pronounced crack), Irish for "fun" or "a good laugh," means good conversation for the participants. It's the sport that accompanies drinking in a pub. People are there to talk. Don't be afraid to make new friends. To toast them in Irish, say, *"Slainte"* (SLAWN-chuh).

Traditional music is alive and popular in pubs throughout Ireland. "Sessions" (musical evenings) may be planned and advertised or impromptu. There's generally a fiddle, a flute or tin whistle, a guitar, a *bodhrán* (goatskin drum), and maybe an accordion or mandolin. Things usually get going at about 21:30. Last call for drinks is at about 23:30.

Transportation

By Car: A car is a worthless headache in Dublin. But if venturing into the countryside, I enjoy the freedom of a rental car for reaching far-flung rural sights. It's cheaper to arrange most car rentals from the US. Note that many credit-card companies do not offer collision coverage for rentals in Ireland. For tips on your insurance options, see www.ricksteves.com/cdw, and for route planning, consult www.viamichelin.com. Bring your driver's license. In the Republic of Ireland, you generally can't rent a car if you're 75 or older, and you'll pay extra if you're 70-74.

Remember that the Irish drive on the left side of the road (and the driver sits on the right side of the car). You'll quickly master Ireland's many roundabouts: Traffic moves clockwise, cars inside the roundabout have the right-of-way, and entering traffic yields (look to your right as you merge). Note that "camera cops" strictly enforce speed limits by automatically snapping photos of speeders' license plates, then mailing them a bill.

Local road etiquette is similar to that in the US. Ask your car-rental company about the rules of the road, or check the US State

Department website (www.travel.state.gov, click on "International Travel," then specify your country of choice and click "Traffic Safety and Road Conditions").

By Train and Bus: You can check train schedules at www.irishrail.ie or listen to a recorded timetable at 01/890-778-899. In Ireland, most travelers find it's cheapest simply to buy train tickets as they go. To see if a railpass could save you money, check www.ricksteves.com/rail.

Long-distance buses (called "coaches") are about a third slower than trains, but they're also much cheaper. Bus stations are normally at or near train stations. The Bus Éireann Expressway Bus Timetable is handy (free, available at some bus stations or online at www.buseireann.ie, bus info tel. 01/836-6111).

Helpful Hints

Emergency Help: To summon the **police** or an **ambulance,** dial 999. For passport problems, call the **US Embassy** (in Dublin, tel. 01/668-7122 or 01/668-8777) or the **Canadian Embassy** (in Dublin, tel. 01/234-4000). For other concerns, get advice from your hotelier.

Theft or Loss: To replace a passport, you'll need to go in person to an embassy or consulate (see above). Cancel and replace your credit and debit cards by calling these 24-hour US numbers collect: Visa—tel. 303/967-1096, MasterCard—tel. 636/722-7111, American Express—tel. 336/393-1111. File a police report either on the spot or within a day or two; you'll need it to submit an insurance claim for lost or stolen railpasses or travel gear, and it can help with replacing your passport or credit and debit cards. Precautionary measures can minimize the effects of loss—back up your digital photos and other files frequently. For more information, see www.ricksteves.com/help.

Time: Ireland uses the 24-hour clock. It's the same through 12:00 noon, then keep going: 13:00, 14:00, and so on. Ireland, like Great Britain, is five/eight hours ahead of the East/West Coasts of the US (and one hour earlier than most of continental Europe).

Holidays and Festivals: Ireland celebrates many holidays, which can close sights and attract crowds (book hotel rooms ahead). For information on holidays and festivals, check Ireland's tourism website: www.discoverireland.com. For a simple list showing major—though not all—events, see www.ricksteves.com/festivals.

Numbers and Stumblers: What Americans call the second floor of a building is the first floor in Ireland. Irish people write dates as day/month/year, so Christmas is 25/12/14. For most measurements, Ireland uses the metric system: A kilogram is 2.2 pounds, and a liter is about a quart. For driving distances, the country is still transitioning from miles to kilometers on some road signs, but the speed limits are now given in kilometers per hour (a kilometer is six-tenths of a mile).

Resources from Rick Steves

This Snapshot guide is excerpted from my latest edition of *Rick Steves' Ireland,* which is one of more than 30 titles in my series of guidebooks on European travel. I also produce a public television series, *Rick Steves' Europe,* and a public radio show, *Travel with Rick Steves.* My website, www.ricksteves.com, offers free travel information, a forum for travelers' comments, guidebook updates, my travel blog, an online travel store, and information on European railpasses and our tours of Europe. If you're bringing a mobile device on your trip, you can download free information from Rick Steves Audio Europe, featuring podcasts of my radio shows, free audio tours of major sights in Europe, and travel interviews about Ireland (via www.ricksteves.com/audioeurope, iTunes, Google Play, or the Rick Steves Audio Europe free smartphone app). You can follow me on Facebook and Twitter.

Additional Resources

Tourist Information: www.discoverireland.com
Passports and Red Tape: www.travel.state.gov
Travel Insurance Tips: www.ricksteves.com/insurance
Packing List: www.ricksteves.com/packlist
Cheap Flights: www.kayak.com
Airplane Carry-on Restrictions: www.tsa.gov/travelers
Updates for This Book: www.ricksteves.com/update

How Was Your Trip?

If you'd like to share your tips, concerns, and discoveries after using this book, please fill out the survey at www.ricksteves.com/feedback. Thanks in advance—it helps a lot.

INDEX

INDEX

INDEX

INDEX

INDEX

Audio Europe™

Rick's Free Travel App

Get your FREE **Rick Steves Audio Europe**™ app to enjoy...

- Dozens of self-guided tours of Europe's top museums, sights and historic walks

- Hundreds of tracks filled with cultural insights and sightseeing tips from Rick's radio interviews

- All organized into handy geographic playlists

- For iPhone, iPad, iPod Touch, Android

With Rick whispering in your ear, Europe gets even better.

Find out more at ricksteves.com

Start your trip at

Free information and great gear to

▶ Explore Europe

Browse thousands of articles, video clips, photos and radio interviews, plus find a wealth of money-saving tips for planning your dream trip. You'll find up-to-date information on Europe's best destinations, packing smart, getting around, finding rooms, staying healthy, avoiding scams and more.

▶ Travel News

Subscribe to our free Travel News e-newsletter, and get monthly updates from Rick on what's happening in Europe!

▶ Travel Forums

Learn, ask, share—our online community of savvy travelers is a great resource for first-time travelers to Europe, as well as seasoned pros.

Rick Steves' Europe Through the Back Door, Inc.

EUROPE GUIDES

Best of Europe
Eastern Europe
Europe Through the Back Door
Mediterranean Cruise Ports
Northern European Cruise Ports

COUNTRY GUIDES

Croatia & Slovenia
England
France
Germany
Great Britain
Ireland
Italy
Portugal
Scandinavia
Spain
Switzerland

CITY & REGIONAL GUIDES

Amsterdam, Bruges & Brussels
Barcelona
Budapest
Florence & Tuscany
Greece: Athens & the Peloponnese
Istanbul
London
Paris
Prague & the Czech Republic
Provence & the French Riviera
Rome
Venice
Vienna, Salzburg & Tirol

SNAPSHOT GUIDES

Basque Country: Spain & France
Berlin
Bruges & Brussels
Copenhagen & the Best of
   Denmark
Dublin
Dubrovnik
Hill Towns of Central Italy
Italy's Cinque Terre
Krakow, Warsaw & Gdansk
Lisbon
Madrid & Toledo
Milan & the Italian Lakes District
Munich, Bavaria & Salzburg
Naples & the Amalfi Coast
Northern Ireland
Norway
Scotland
Sevilla, Granada & Southern Spain
Stockholm

POCKET GUIDES

Amsterdam
Athens
Barcelona
Florence
London
Paris
Rome
Venice

Rick Steves guidebooks are published by Avalon Travel,
a member of the Perseus Books Group.

NOW AVAILABLE:
eBOOKS, DVD & BLU-RAY

TRAVEL CULTURE

Europe 101
European Christmas
Postcards from Europe
Travel as a Political Act

eBOOKS

*Nearly all Rick Steves guides are
available as ebooks. Check with
your favorite bookseller.*

RICK STEVES' EUROPE DVDs

11 New Shows 2013–2014
Austria & the Alps
Eastern Europe
England & Wales
European Christmas
European Travel Skills & Specials
France
Germany, BeNeLux & More
Greece, Turkey & Portugal
Iran
Ireland & Scotland
Italy's Cities
Italy's Countryside
Scandinavia
Spain
Travel Extras

BLU-RAY

Celtic Charms
Eastern Europe Favorites
European Christmas
Italy Through the Back Door
Mediterranean Mosaic
Surprising Cities of Europe

PHRASE BOOKS & DICTIONARIES

French
French, Italian & German
German
Italian
Portuguese
Spanish

JOURNALS

Rick Steves Pocket Travel Journal
Rick Steves Travel Journal

PLANNING MAPS

Britain, Ireland & London
Europe
France & Paris
Germany, Austria & Switzerland
Ireland
Italy
Spain & Portugal

RickSteves.com 🅕🅣 @RickSteves

Rick Steves books and DVDs are available at bookstores
and through online booksellers.

Photo © Patricia Feaster

Avalon Travel
a member of the Perseus Books Group
1700 Fourth Street
Berkeley, CA 94710

Text © 2013 by Rick Steves.
Maps © 2013 by Europe Through the Back Door.
Printed in Canada by Friesens.
Second printing October 2014.
Portions of this book originally appeared in *Rick Steves' Ireland 2014*.

ISBN 978-1-61238-690-4

For the latest on Rick's lectures, guidebooks, tours, public radio show, and public television series, contact Europe Through the Back Door, Box 2009, Edmonds, WA 98020, tel. 425/771-8303, www.ricksteves.com, rick@ricksteves.com.

Europe Through the Back Door

Managing Editor: Risa Laib
Editorial & Production Manager: Jennifer Madison Davis
Editors: Glenn Eriksen, Tom Griffin, Cameron Hewitt, Deb Jensen, Suzanne Kotz, Cathy Lu, John Pierce, Carrie Shepherd
Editorial Assistant: Jessica Shaw
Editorial Intern: Zosha Milliman
Maps & Graphics: David C. Hoerlein, Lauren Mills, Dawn Tessman Visser, Laura VanDeventer

Avalon Travel

Senior Editor and Series Manager: Madhu Prasher
Editor: Jamie Andrade
Associate Editor: Annette Kohl
Assistant Editor: Maggie Ryan
Copy Editor: Denise Silva
Proofreader: Janet Walden
Indexer: Stephen Callahan
Cover Design: Kimberly Glyder Design
Maps & Graphics: Kat Bennett, Mike Morgenfeld

Cover Photo: Temple Bar in Dublin © Gergo Kazsimer/Dreamstime.com
Title Page Photo: the Temple Bar district in Dublin, Ireland © Patricia Hofmeester/ www.123rf.co
Page 1 Photo: statue of Oscar Wilde, in Merrion Square Park, Dublin © Brenda Kean/123rf.com
Additional Photography: Pat O'Connor, Rick Steves, David C. Hoerlein, Dominic Bonuccelli, Wikimedia Commons

ABOUT THE AUTHORS

RICK STEVES

 Since 1973, Rick Steves has spent 100 days every year exploring Europe. Along with writing and researching a bestselling series of guidebooks, Rick produces a public television series *(Rick Steves' Europe)*, a public radio show *(Travel with Rick Steves)*, a blog (on Facebook), and an app and podcast *(Rick Steves Audio Europe)*; writes a nationally syndicated newspaper column; organizes guided tours that take over 15,000 travelers to Europe annually; and offers an information-packed website (www.ricksteves.com). With the help of his hardworking staff of 90 at Europe Through the Back Door—in Edmonds, Washington, just north of Seattle—Rick's mission is to make European travel fun, affordable, and culturally enlightening for Americans.

Connect with Rick:

 facebook.com/RickSteves  twitter: @RickSteves

PAT O'CONNOR

 Pat O'Connor, an Irish-American, first journeyed to Ireland in 1981 and was hooked by the history and passion of the feisty Irish culture. Frequent return visits led to his partnership with Rick, his work as an Ireland tour guide for Rick Steves' Europe Through the Back Door, and co-authorship of this book. Pat, who loves all things Hibernian except the black pudding, thrives on the adventures that occur as he slogs the bogs and drives the Irish back lanes (more than 2,000 kilometers annually) in search of new discoveries.

Want More Ireland?
Maximize the experience with Rick Steves as your guide

Guidebooks
London and Britain guides make side-trips smooth and affordable

Planning Maps
Use the map that's in sync with your guidebook

Rick's DVDs
Preview your destinations with 4 shows on Ireland

Free! Rick's Audio Europe™ App
Hear Ireland travel tips from Rick's radio shows

Small-Group Tours
Take a lively Rick Steves tour through Ireland

For all the details, visit ricksteves.com